A Prentice Hall Pocket Reader

PURPOSES

Edited by

Stephen P. Reid
Colorado State University

PEARSON

Prentice
Hall

Upper Saddle River, New Jersey 07458

© 2007 by PEARSON EDUCATION, INC.
Upper Saddle River, New Jersey 07458

ISBN 0-13-228161-9

Printed in the United States of America

CONTENTS

1

OBSERVING

LENSES

Annie Dillard

You get used to looking through lenses; it is an acquired skill. 1
When you first look through binoculars, for instance, you can't see a
thing. You look at the inside of the barrel; you blink and watch your
eyelashes; you play with the focus knob till one eye is purblind.

The microscope is even worse. You are supposed to keep both 2
eyes open as you look through its single eyepiece. I spent my childhood in Pittsburgh trying to master this trick: seeing through one
eye, with both eyes open. The microscope also teaches you to move
your hands wrong, to shove the glass slide to the right if you are following a creature who is swimming off to the left—as if you were
operating a tiller, or backing a trailer, or performing any other of
those paradoxical maneuvers which require either sure instincts or a
grasp of elementary physics, neither of which I possess.

A child's microscope set comes with a little five-watt lamp. You 3
place this dim light in front of the microscope's mirror; the mirror
bounces the light up through the slide, through the magnifying
lenses, and into your eye. The only reason you do not see everything
in silhouette is that microscopic things are so small they are translucent. The animals and plants in a drop of pond water pass light like
pale stained glass; they seem so soaked in water and light that their
opacity has leached away.

The translucent strands of algae you see under a microscope— 4
Spirogyra, Oscillatoria, Cladophora—move of their own accord, no
one knows how or why. You watch these swaying yellow, green, and
brown strands of algae half mesmerized; you sink into the microscope's field forgetful, oblivious, as if it were all a dream of your

1

deepest brain. Occasionally a zippy rotifer comes barreling through, black and white, and in a tremendous hurry.

My rotifers and daphniae and amoebae were in an especially ⁵ tremendous hurry because they were drying up. I burnt out or broke my little five-watt bulb right away. To replace it, I rigged an old table lamp laid on its side; the table lamp carried a seventy-five-watt bulb. I was about twelve, immortal and invulnerable, and did not know what I was doing; neither did anyone else. My parents let me set up my laboratory in the basement, where they wouldn't have to smell the urine I collected in test tubes and kept in the vain hope it would grow something horrible. So in full, solitary ignorance I spent evenings in the basement staring into a seventy-five-watt bulb magnified three hundred times and focused into my eye. It is a wonder I can see at all. My eyeball itself would start drying up; I blinked and blinked.

But the pond water creatures fared worse. I dropped them on a ⁶ slide, floated a cover slip over them, and laid the slide on the microscope's stage, which the seventy-five-watt bulb had heated like a grill. At once the drop of pond water started to evaporate. Its edges shrank. The creatures swam among algae in a diminishing pool. I liked this part. The heat worked for me as a centrifuge, to concentrate the biomass. I had about five minutes to watch the members of a very dense population, excited by the heat, go about their business until— as I fancied sadly—they all caught on to their situation and started making out wills.

I was, then, not only watching the much-vaunted wonders in a ⁷ drop of pond water; I was also, with mingled sadism and sympathy, setting up a limitless series of apocalypses. I set up and staged hundreds of ends-of-the-world and watched, enthralled, as they played themselves out. Over and over again, the last trump sounded, the final scroll unrolled, and the known world drained, dried, and vanished. When all the creatures lay motionless, boiled and fried in the positions they had when the last of their water dried completely, I washed the slide in the sink and started over with a fresh drop. How I loved that deep, wet world where the colored algae waved in the water and the rotifers swam!

But oddly, this is a story about swans. It is not even a story; it is ⁸ a description of swans. This description of swans includes the sky over a pond, a pair of binoculars, and a mortal adult who had long since moved out of the Pittsburgh basement.

In the Roanoke valley of Virginia, rimmed by the Blue Ridge ⁹ Mountains to the east and the Allegheny Mountains to the west, is a little semiagricultural area called Daleville. In Daleville, set among fallow fields and wooded ridges, is Daleville Pond. It is a big pond, maybe ten acres; it holds a lot of sky. I used to haunt the place because I loved it; I still do. In winter it had that airy scruffiness of deciduous lands; you greet the daylight and the open space, and spend the evening picking burrs out of your pants.

One Valentine's Day, in the afternoon, I was crouched among dried reeds at the edge of Daleville Pond. Across the pond from where I crouched was a low forested mountain ridge. In every other direction I saw only sky, sky crossed by the reeds which blew before my face whichever way I turned.

I was looking through binoculars at a pair of whistling swans. Whistling swans! It is impossible to say how excited I was to see whistling swans in Daleville, Virginia. The two were a pair, mated for life, migrating north and west from the Atlantic coast to the high arctic. They had paused to feed at Daleville Pond. I had flushed them, and now they were flying and circling the pond. I crouched in the reeds so they would not be afraid to come back to the water.

Through binoculars I followed the swans, swinging where they flew. All their feathers were white; their eyes were black. Their wingspan was six feet; they were bigger than I was. They flew in unison, one behind the other; they made pass after pass at the pond. I watched them change from white swans in front of the mountain to black swans in front of the sky. In clockwise ellipses they flew, necks long and relaxed, alternately beating their wide wings and gliding.

As I rotated on my heels to keep the black frame of the lenses around them, I lost all sense of space. If I lowered the binoculars I was always amazed to learn in which direction I faced—dazed, the way you emerge awed from a movie and try to reconstruct, bit by bit, a real world, in order to discover where in it you might have parked the car.

I lived in that circle of light, in great speed and utter silence. When the swans passed before the sun they were distant—two black threads, two live stitches. But they kept coming smoothly, and the sky deepened to blue behind them and they took on light. They gathered dimension as they neared, and I could see their ardent, straining eyes. Then I could hear the brittle blur of their wings, the blur which faded as they circled on, and the sky brightened to yellow behind them and the swans flattened and darkened and diminished as they flew. Once I lost them behind the mountain ridge; when they emerged they were flying suddenly very high, and it was like music changing key.

I was lost. The reeds in front of me, swaying and out of focus in ₁₅ the binoculars' circular field, were translucent. The reeds were strands of color passing light like cells in water. They were those yellow and green and brown strands of pond algae I had watched so long in a light-soaked field. My eyes burned; I was watching algae wave in a shrinking drop; they crossed each other and parted wetly. And suddenly into the field swam two whistling swans, two tiny whistling swans. They swam as fast as rotifers: two whistling swans, infinitesimal, beating their tiny wet wings, perfectly formed.

TOYS

Roland Barthes

French toys: One could not find a better illustration of the fact 1
that the adult Frenchman sees the child as another self. All the toys
one commonly sees are essentially a microcosm of the adult world;
they are all reduced copies of human objects, as if in the eyes of the
public the child was, all told, nothing but a smaller man, a homuncu-
lus to whom must be supplied objects of his own size.

Invented forms are very rare: a few sets of blocks, which appeal 2
to the spirit of do-it-yourself, are the only ones which offer dynamic
forms. As for the others, French toys *always mean something*, and this
something is always entirely socialized, constituted by the myths or
the techniques of modern adult life: the army, broadcasting, the post
office, medicine (miniature instrument-cases, operating theaters for
dolls), school, hair styling (driers for permanent-waving), the air
force (parachutists), transport (trains, Citroëns, Vedettes, Vespas,
petrol stations), science (Martian toys).

The fact that French toys *literally* prefigure the world of adult 3
functions obviously cannot but prepare the child to accept them all,
by constituting for him, even before he can think about it, the alibi of
a Nature which has at all times created soldiers, postmen, and
Vespas. Toys here reveal the list of all the things the adult does not
find unusual: war, bureaucracy, ugliness, Martians, etc. It is not so
much, in fact, the imitation which is the sign of an abdication, as its
literalness: French toys are like a Jivaro head, in which one recog-
nizes, shrunken to the size of an apple, the wrinkles and hair of an
adult. There exist, for instance, dolls which urinate; they have an
esophagus, one gives them a bottle, they wet their nappies; soon, no
doubt, milk will turn to water in their stomachs. This is meant to prepare the little girl for the causality of housekeeping, to "condition"
her to her future role as mother. However, faced with this world of
faithful and complicated objects, the child can only identify himself
as owner, as user, never as creator; he does not invent the world, he
uses it: There are, prepared for him, actions without adventure, without wonder, without joy. He is turned into a little stay-at-home
householder who does not even have to invent the mainsprings of
adult causality; they are supplied to him ready-made: He has only to
help himself, he is never allowed to discover anything from start to
finish. The merest set of blocks, provided it is not too refined, implies

a very different learning of the world: Then, the child does not in any way create meaningful objects, it matters little to him whether they have an adult name; the actions he performs are not those of a user but those of a demiurge. He creates forms which walk, which roll, he creates life, not property: Objects now act by themselves, they are no longer an inert and complicated material in the palm of his hand. But such toys are rather rare: French toys are usually based on imitation, they are meant to produce children who are users, not creators.

The bourgeois status of toys can be recognized not only in their   4
forms, which are all functional, but also in their substances. Current toys are made of a graceless material, the product of chemistry, not of nature. Many are now molded from complicated mixtures; the plastic material of which they are made has an appearance at once gross and hygienic, it destroys all the pleasure, the sweetness, the humanity of touch. A sign which fills one with consternation is the gradual disappearance of wood, in spite of its being an ideal material because of its firmness and its softness, and the natural warmth of its touch. Wood removes, from all the forms which it supports, the wounding quality of angles which are too sharp, the chemical coldness of metal. When the child handles it and knocks it, it neither vibrates nor grates, it has a sound at once muffled and sharp. It is a familiar and poetic substance, which does not sever the child from close contact with the tree, the table, the floor. Wood does not wound or break down; it does not shatter, it wears out, it can last a long time, live with the child, alter little by little the relations between the object and the hand. If it dies, it is in dwindling, not in swelling out like those mechanical toys which disappear behind the hernia of a broken spring. Wood makes essential objects, objects for all time. Yet there hardly remain any of these wooden toys from the Vosges, these fretwork farms with their animals, which were only possible, it is true, in the days of the craftsman. Henceforth, toys are chemical in substance and color; their very material introduces one to a coenaesthesis of use, not pleasure. These toys die in fact very quickly, and once dead, they have no posthumous life for the child.

BARBIE AT 35

Anna Quindlen

My theory is that to get rid of Barbie you'd have to drive a silver 1
stake through her plastic heart. Or a silver lamé stake, the sort of
thing that might accompany Barbie's Dream Tent.

This is not simply because the original Barbie, launched lo these 2
35 years ago, was more than a little vampiric in appearance, more
Natasha of "Rocky and Bullwinkle" than the "ultimate girl next
door" Mattel describes in her press kit.

It's not only that Barbie, like Dracula, can appear in guises that 3
mask her essential nature: Surgeon, Astronaut, Unicef Ambassador.
Or that she is untouched by time, still the same parody of the female
form she's been since 1959. She's said by her manufacturers to be
"eleven and one-half stylish inches" tall. If she were a real live
woman she would not have enough body fat to menstruate regularly.
Which may be why there's no PMS Barbie.

The silver stake is necessary because Barbie—the issue, not the 4
doll—simply will not be put to rest.

"Mama, why can't I have Barbie?" 5

"Because I hate Barbie. She gives little girls the message that the 6
only thing that's important is being tall and thin and having a big
chest and lots of clothes. She's a terrible role model."

"Oh, Mama, don't be silly. She's just a toy." 7

It's an excellent comeback; if only it were accurate. But consider 8
the recent study at the University of Arizona investigating the attitudes of white and black teen-age girls toward body image.

The attitudes of the white girls were a nightmare. Ninety percent 9
expressed dissatisfaction with their own bodies and many said they
saw dieting as a kind of all-purpose panacea. "I think the reason I
would diet would be to gain self-confidence," said one. "I'd feel like
it was a way of getting control," said another.

And they were curiously united in their description of the perfect 10
girl. She's 5 feet 7 inches, weighs just over 100 pounds, has long legs
and flowing hair. The researchers concluded, "The ideal girl was a
living manifestation of the Barbie doll."

While the white girls described an impossible ideal, black teen- 11
agers talked about appearance in terms of style, attitude, pride and
personality. White respondents talked "thin," black ones "shapely."
Seventy percent of the black teen-agers said they were satisfied with

their weight, and there was little emphasis on dieting. "We're all brought up and taught to be realistic about life," said one, "and we don't look at things the way you want them to be. You look at them the way they are."

There's a quiet irony in that. While black women correctly complain that they are not sufficiently represented in advertisements, commercials, movies, even dolls, perhaps the scarcity of those idealized and unrealistic models may help in some fashion to liberate black teen-agers from ridiculous standards of appearance. When the black teen-agers were asked about the ideal woman, many asked: Whose ideal? The perfect girl projected by the white world simply didn't apply to them or their community, which set beauty standards from within. "White girls," one black participant in the Arizona study wrote, "have to look like Barbie dolls."   12

There are lots of reasons teen-age girls have such a distorted funhouse mirror image of their own bodies, so distorted that one study found that 83 percent wanted to lose weight, although 62 percent were in the normal range. Fashion designers still showcase anorexia chic; last year the supermodel Kate Moss was reduced to insisting that, yes, she did eat.   13

But long before Kate and Ultra Slimfast came along, hanging over the lives of every little girl born in the second half of the twentieth century was the impossible curvy shadow (40-18-32 in life-size terms) of Barbie. That preposterous physique, we learn as kids, is what a woman looks like with her clothes off. "Two Barbie dolls are sold every second," says Barbie's résumé, which is more extensive than that of Hillary Rodham Clinton. "Barbie doll has had more than a billion pairs of shoes . . . has had over 500 professional makeovers . . . has become the most popular toy ever created."   14

Has been single-handedly responsible for the popularity of the silicone implant?   15

Maybe, as my daughter suggests while she whines in her Barbie-free zone, that's too much weight to put on something that's just a toy. Maybe not. Happy birthday, Babs. Have a piece of cake. Have two.   16

The San Francisco Earthquake

Jack London

The earthquake shook down in San Francisco hundreds of thousands of dollars' worth of walls and chimneys. But the conflagration that followed burned up hundreds of millions of dollars' worth of property. There is no estimating within hundreds of millions the actual damage wrought. Not in history has a modern imperial city been so completely destroyed. San Francisco is gone. Nothing remains of it but memories and a fringe of dwelling-houses on its outskirts. Its industrial section is wiped out. Its business section is wiped out. The factories and warehouses, the great stores and newspaper buildings, the hotels and the palaces of the nabobs, are all gone. Remains only the fringe of dwelling-houses on the outskirts of what was once San Francisco.

Within an hour after the earthquake shock the smoke of San Francisco's burning was a lurid tower visible a hundred miles away. And for three days and nights this lurid tower swayed in the sky, reddening the sun, darkening the day, and filling the land with smoke.

On Wednesday morning at a quarter past five came the earthquake. A minute later the flames were leaping upward. In a dozen different quarters south of Market Street, in the working-class ghetto, and in the factories, fires started. There was no opposing the flames. There was no organization, no communication. All the cunning adjustments of a twentieth-century city had been smashed by the earthquake. The streets were humped into ridges and depressions, and piled with the debris of fallen walls. The steel rails were twisted into perpendicular and horizontal angles. The telephone and telegraph systems were disrupted. And the great water-mains had burst. All the shrewd contrivances and safe-guards of man had been thrown out of gear by thirty seconds' twitching of the earth-crust.

The Fire Made Its Own Draft

By Wednesday afternoon, inside of twelve hours, half the heart of the city was gone. At that time I watched the vast conflagration from out on the bay. It was dead calm. Not a flicker of wind stirred. Yet from every side wind was pouring in upon the city. East, west, north, and south, strong winds were blowing upon the doomed city. The heated air rising made an enormous suck. Thus did the fire of itself build its own colossal chimney through the atmosphere. Day and night this dead calm continued, and yet, near to the flames, the wind was often half a gale, so mighty was the suck.

Wednesday night saw the destruction of the very heart of the 5 city. Dynamite was lavishly used, and many of San Francisco's proudest structures were crumbled by man himself into ruins, but there was no withstanding the onrush of the flames. Time and again successful stands were made by the fire-fighters, and every time the flames flanked around on either side, or came up from the rear, and turned to defeat the hard-won victory.

An enumeration of the buildings destroyed would be a directory 6 of San Francisco. An enumeration of the buildings undestroyed would be a line and several addresses. An enumeration of the deeds of heroism would stock a library and bankrupt the Carnegie Medal fund. An enumeration of the dead will never be made. All vestiges of them were destroyed by the flames. The number of victims of the earthquake will never be known. South of Market Street, where the loss of life was particularly heavy, was the first to catch fire.

Remarkable as it may seem, Wednesday night, while the whole 7 city crashed and roared into ruin, was a quiet night. There were no crowds. There was no shouting and yelling. There was no hysteria, no disorder. I passed Wednesday night in the path of the advancing flames, and in all those terrible hours I saw not one woman who wept, not one man who was excited, not one person who was in the slightest degree panic-stricken.

Before the flames, throughout the night, fled tens of thousands of 8 homeless ones. Some were wrapped in blankets. Others carried bundles of bedding and dear household treasures. Sometimes a whole family was harnessed to a carriage or delivery wagon that was weighted down with their possessions. Baby buggies, toy wagons, and go-carts were used as trucks, while every other person was dragging a trunk. Yet everybody was gracious. The most perfect courtesy obtained. Never, in all San Francisco's history, were her people so kind and courteous as on this night of terror.

A Caravan of Trunks

All night these tens of thousands fled before the flames. Many of 9 them, the poor people from the labor ghetto, had fled all day as well. They had left their homes burdened with possessions. Now and again they lightened up, flinging out upon the street clothing and treasures they had dragged for miles.

They held on longest to their trunks, and over these trunks many 10 a strong man broke his heart that night. The hills of San Francisco are steep, and up these hills, mile after mile, were the trunks dragged. Everywhere were trunks, with across them lying their exhausted owners, men and women. Before the march of the flames were flung picket lines of soldiers. And a block at a time, as the flames advanced, these pickets retreated. One of their tasks was to keep the trunk-pullers moving. The exhausted creatures, stirred on by the menace of bayonets, would arise and struggle up the steep pavements, pausing from weakness every five or ten feet.

Often, after surmounting a heart-breaking hill, they would find 11 another wall of flame advancing upon them at right angles and be compelled to change anew the line of their retreat. In the end, completely played out, after toiling for a dozen hours like giants, thousands of them were compelled to abandon their trunks. Here the shopkeepers and soft members of the middle class were at a disadvantage. But the working men dug holes in vacant lots and backyards and buried their trunks.

The Doomed City

At nine o'clock Wednesday evening I walked down through the 12 very heart of the city. I walked through miles and miles of magnificent buildings and towering skyscrapers. Here was no fire. All was in perfect order. The police patrolled the streets. Every building had its watchman at the door. And yet it was doomed, all of it. There was no water. The dynamite was giving out. And at right angles two different conflagrations were sweeping down upon it.

At one o'clock in the morning I walked down through the 13 same section. Everything still stood intact. There was no fire. And yet there was a change. A rain of ashes was falling. The watchmen at the doors were gone. The police had been withdrawn. There were no firemen, no fire engines, no men fighting with dynamite. The district had been absolutely abandoned. I stood at the corner of Kearney and Market, in the very innermost heart of San Francisco. Kearney Street was deserted. Half a dozen blocks away it was burning on both sides. The street was a wall of flame, and against this wall of flame, silhouetted sharply, were two United States cavalrymen sitting their horses, calmly watching. That was all. Not another person was in sight. In the intact heart of the city two troopers sat their horses and watched.

Spread of the Conflagration

Surrender was complete. There was no water. The sewers had [14] long since been pumped dry. There was no dynamite. Another fire had broken out further uptown, and now from three sides conflagrations were sweeping down. The fourth side had been burned earlier in the day. In that direction stood the tottering walls of the Examiner building, the burned-out Call building, the smoldering ruins of the Grand Hotel, and the gutted, devastated, dynamited Palace Hotel.

The following will illustrate the sweep of the flames and the [15] inability of men to calculate their spread. At eight o'clock Wednesday evening I passed through Union Square. It was packed with refugees. Thousands of them had gone to bed on the grass.

Government tents had been set up, supper was being cooked, [16] and the refugees were lining up for free meals.

At half-past one in the morning three sides of Union Square were [17] in flames. The fourth side, where stood the great St. Francis Hotel, was still holding out. An hour later, ignited from top and sides, the St. Francis was flaming heavenward. Union Square, heaped high with mountains of trunks, was deserted. Troops, refugees, and all had retreated.

A Fortune for a Horse!

It was at Union Square that I saw a man offering a thousand dol- [18] lars for a team of horses. He was in charge of a truck piled high with trunks for some hotel. It had been hauled here into what was considered safety, and the horses had been taken out. The flames were on three sides of the Square, and there were no horses.

Also, at this time, standing beside the truck, I urged a man to [19] seek safety in flight. He was all but hemmed in by several conflagrations. He was an old man and he was on crutches. Said he, "Today is my birthday. Last night I was worth thirty thousand dollars. I bought five bottles of wine, some delicate fish, and other things for my birthday dinner. I have had no dinner, and all I own are these crutches."

I convinced him of his danger and started him limping on his [20] way. An hour later, from a distance, I saw the truckload of trunks burning merrily in the middle of the street.

On Thursday morning, at a quarter past five, just twenty-four [21] hours after the earthquake, I sat on the steps of a small residence on Nob Hill. With me sat Japanese, Italians, Chinese, and Negroes—a bit of the cosmopolitan flotsam of the wreck of the city. All about were the palaces of the nabob pioneers of Forty-nine. To the east and south, at right angles, were advancing two mighty walls of flame.

I went inside with the owner of the house on the steps of which 22 I sat. He was cool and cheerful and hospitable. "Yesterday morning," he said, "I was worth six hundred thousand dollars. This morning this house is all I have left. It will go in fifteen minutes." He pointed to a large cabinet. "That is my wife's collection of china. This rug upon which we stand is a present. It cost fifteen hundred dollars. Try that piano. Listen to its tone. There are few like it. There are no horses. The flames will be here in fifteen minutes."

Outside, the old Mark Hopkins residence, a palace, was just 23 catching fire. The troops were falling back and driving the refugees before them. From every side came the roaring of flames, the crashing of walls, and the detonations of dynamite.

The Dawn of the Second Day

I passed out of the house. Day was trying to dawn through the 24 smoke-pall. A sickly light was creeping over the face of things. Once only the sun broke through the smoke-pall, blood-red, and showing a quarter its usual size. The smoke-pall itself, viewed from beneath, was a rose color that pulsed and fluttered with lavender shades. Then it turned to mauve and yellow and dun. There was no sun. And so dawned the second day on stricken San Francisco.

An hour later I was creeping past the shattered dome of the City 25 Hall. Than it, there was no better exhibit of the destructive forces of the earthquake. Most of the stone had been shaken from the great dome, leaving standing the naked framework of steel. Market Street was piled high with wreckage, and across the wreckage lay the overthrown pillars of the City Hall shattered into short crosswise sections.

This section of the city, with the exception of the Mint and the 26 Post-Office, was already a waste of smoking ruins. Here and there through the smoke, creeping warily under the shadows of tottering walls, emerged occasional men and women. It was like the meeting of the handful of survivors after the day of the end of the world.

Beeves Slaughtered and Roasted

On Mission Street lay a dozen steers, in a neat row stretching 27 across the street, just as they had been struck down by the flying ruins of the earthquake. The fire had passed through afterward and roasted them. The human dead had been carried away before the fire came. At another place on Mission Street I saw a milk wagon. A steel telegraph pole had smashed down sheer through the driver's seat and crushed the front wheels. The milkcans lay scattered around.

All day Thursday and all Thursday night, all day Friday and Friday night, the flames still raged. 28

Friday night saw the flames finally conquered, though not until Russian Hill and Telegraph Hill had been swept and three-quarters of a mile of wharves and docks had been licked up. 29

The Last Stand

The great stand of the fire-fighters was made Thursday night on Van Ness Avenue. Had they failed here, the comparatively few remaining houses of the city would have been swept. Here were the magnificent residences of the second generation of San Francisco nabobs, and these, in a solid zone, were dynamited down across the path of the fire. Here and there the flames leaped the zone, but these fires were beaten out, principally by the use of wet blankets and rugs. 30

San Francisco, at the present time, is like the crater of a volcano, around which are camped tens of thousand of refugees. At the Presidio alone are at least twenty thousand. All the surrounding cities and towns are jammed with the homeless ones, where they are being cared for by the relief committees. The refugees were carried free by the railroads to any point they wished to go, and it is estimated that over one hundred thousand people have left the peninsula on which San Francisco stood. The Government has the situation in hand, and, thanks to the immediate relief given by the whole United States, there is not the slightest possibility of a famine. The bankers and business men have already set about making preparations to rebuild San Francisco. 31

2

REMEMBERING

MARINA

Judith Ortiz Cofer

Again it happened between my mother and me. Since her return 1 to Puerto Rico after my father's death ten years before, she had gone totally "native," regressing into the comfortable traditions of her extended family and questioning all of my decisions. Each year we spoke more formally to each other, and each June, at the end of my teaching year, she would invite me to visit her on the Island—so I could see for myself how much I was missing out on.

These yearly pilgrimages to my mother's town where I had been 2 born also, but which I had left at an early age, were for me symbolic of the clash of cultures and generations that she and I represent. But I looked forward to arriving at this lovely place, my mother's lifetime dream of home, now endangered by encroaching "progress."

Located on the west coast, our pueblo is a place of contrasts: the 3 original town remains as a tiny core of ancient houses circling the church, which sits on a hill, the very same where the woodcutter claimed to have been saved from a charging bull by a lovely dark Lady who appeared floating over a treetop. There my mother lives, at the foot of this hill; but surrounding this postcard scene there are shopping malls, a Burger King, a cinema. And where the sugar cane fields once extended like a green sea as far as the eye could see: condominiums, cement blocks in rows, all the same shape and color. My mother tries not to see this part of her world. The church bells drown the noise of traffic, and when she sits on her back porch and looks up at the old church built by the hands of generations of men whose last names she would not recognize, she feels safe—under the shelter of the past.

During the twenty years she spent in "exile" in the U.S. often   4
alone with two children, waiting for my father, she dedicated her
time and energy to creating a "reasonable facsimile" of a Puerto
Rican home, which for my brother and me meant that we led a dual
existence: speaking Spanish at home with her, acting out our parts in
her traditional play, while also daily pretending assimilation in the
classroom, where in the early sixties, there was no such thing as bilin-
gual education. But, to be fair, we were not the only Puerto Rican
children leading a double life, and I have always been grateful to
have kept my Spanish. My trouble with Mother comes when she and
I try to define and translate key words for both of us, words such as
"woman" and "mother." I have a daughter too, as well as a demand-
ing profession as a teacher and writer. My mother got married as a
teenager and led a life of isolation and total devotion to her duties as
mother. As a Penelope-like wife, she was always waiting, waiting,
waiting, for the return of her sailor, for the return to her native land.

In the meantime, I grew up in the social flux of the sixties in New   5
Jersey, and although I was kept on a steady diet of fantasies about life
in the tropics, I liberated myself from her plans for me, got a scholarship to college, married a man who supported my need to work, to
create, to travel and to experience life as an individual. My mother
rejoices at my successes, but is often anxious at how much time I
have to spend away from home, although I keep assuring her that
my husband is as good a parent as I am, and a much better cook. Her
concern about my familial duties is sometimes a source of friction in
our relationship, the basis for most of our arguments. But, in spite of
our differences, I miss her, and as June approaches, I yearn to be with
her in her tiny house filled with her vibrant presence. So I pack up
and go to meet my loving adversary in her corner of the rapidly dis-
appearing "paradise" that she waited so long to go home to.

It was after a heated argument one afternoon that I sought rec-   6
onciliation with my mother by asking her to go with me for a walk
down the main street of the pueblo. I planned to request stories about
the town and its old people, something that we both enjoy for different reasons: she likes recalling the old days, and I have an insatiable
curiosity about the history and the people of the Island which have
become prominent features in my work.

We had been walking around the church when we saw a distin-   7
guished looking old man strolling hand-in-hand with a little girl. My
mother touched my arm and pointed to them. I admired the pair as
the old man, svelte and graceful as a ballet dancer, lifted the tiny figure dressed up in pink lace onto a stool at an outdoor cafe.

"Who is he?" I asked my mother, trying not to stare as we pre- 8
tended to examine the menu taped on the window.

"You have heard his story at your grandmother's house." 9

She took my elbow and led me to a table at the far end of the cafe. 10
"I will tell it to you again, but first I will give you a hint about who
he is: he has not always been the man he is today."

Though her "hint" was no help, I suddenly recalled the story I 11
had heard many years earlier as told by my grandmother, who had
started the tale with similar words, "People are not always what they
seem to be, that is something we have all heard, but have you heard
about the one who ended up being what he was but did not appear
to be?" Or something like that. Mamá could turn any story—it did
not have to be as strange and fascinating as this one—into an event.
I told my guess to my mother.

"Yes," she nodded, "he came home to retire. You know he has 12
lived in Nueva York since before you were born. Do you remember
the story?"

As we continued our walk, my mother recounted for me her 13
mother's dramatic tale of a famous incident that had shaken the
town in Mamá's youth. I had heard it once as a child, sitting
enthralled at my grandmother's knee.

In the days when Mamá was a young girl, our pueblo had not yet 14
been touched by progress. The cult of the Black Virgin had grown
strong as pilgrims traveled from all over the island to visit the shrine,
and the Church preached chastity and modesty as the prime virtues
for the town's daughters. Adolescent girls were not allowed to go
anywhere without their mothers or *dueñas*—except to a certain river
that no man was allowed to approach.

Río Rojo, the river that ran its course around the sacred mountain 15
where the Virgin had appeared, was reserved for the maidens of the
pueblo. It was nothing but a stream, really, but crystalline, and it was
bordered by thick woods where the most fragrant flowers and herbs
could be found. This was a female place, a pastoral setting where no
true *macho* would want to be caught swimming or fishing.

Nature had decorated the spot like a boudoir—royal poincianas 16
extended their low branches for the girls to hang their clothes, and
the mossy grass grew like a plush green carpet all the way down to
the smooth stepping-stones where they could sun themselves like
favoritas in a virginal harem.

As a "grown" girl of fifteen, Mamá had led her sisters and other 17
girls of the pueblo to bathe there on hot summer afternoons. It was a
place of secret talk and rowdy play, of freedom from mothers and

chaperones, a place where they could talk about boys, and where they could luxuriate in their bodies. At the río, the young women felt free to hypothesize about the secret connection between their two concerns: their changing bodies and boys.

Sex was the forbidden topic in their lives, yet these were the same girls who would be given to strangers in marriage before they were scarcely out of childhood. In a sense, they were betrayed by their own protective parents who could bring themselves to explain neither the delights, nor the consequences of sex to their beloved daughters. The prevailing practice was to get them safely married as soon after puberty as possible—because nature would take its course one way or another. Scandal was to be avoided at all costs.

At the río, the group of girls Mamá grew up with would squeal and splash away their last few precious days as children. They would also wash each other's hair while sitting like brown nyads upon the smooth rocks in the shallow water. They had the freedom to bathe nude, but some of them could not break through a lifetime of training in modesty and would keep their chemises and bloomers on. One of the shyest girls was Marina. She was everyone's pet.

Marina was a lovely young girl with her *café-con-leche* skin and green eyes. Her body was willowy and her thick black Indian hair hung down to her waist. Her voice was so soft that you had to come very close to hear what she was saying during the rare times when she did speak. Everyone treated Marina with special consideration, since she had already known much tragedy by the time she reached adolescence. It was due to the traumatic circumstances of her birth, as well as her difficult life with a reclusive mother, all the girls believed, that Marina was so withdrawn and melancholy as she ended her fifteenth year. She was surely destined for convent life, they all whispered when Marina left their company, as she often did, to go sit by herself on the bank, and to watch them with her large, wet, melancholy eyes.

Marina had fine hands and all the girls liked for her to braid their hair at the end of the day. They argued over the privilege of sitting between her legs while Marina ran her long fingers through their hair like a cellist playing a soothing melody. It caused much jealousy that last summer before Mamá's betrothal (which meant it was the last summer she could play at the río with her friends) when Marina chose to keep company only with Kiki, the mayor's fourteen-year-old daughter who had finally won permission from her strict parents to bathe with the pueblo's girls at the river.

Kiki would be a pale fish among the golden tadpoles in the water. She came from a Spanish family who believed in keeping the bloodlines pure, and she had spent all of her childhood in the cool shade of mansions and convent schools. She had come to the pueblo to prepare for her debut into society, her *quinceañera*, a fifteenth birth-day party where she would be dressed like a princess and displayed before the Island's eligible bachelors as a potential bride.

Lonely for the company of girls her age, and tired of the modu-lated tones of afternoons on the verandah with her refined mother, Kiki had pressured her father to give her a final holiday with the other girls, whom she would see going by the mansion, singing and laughing on their way to the río. Her father began to see the wisdom of her idea when she mentioned how democratic it would seem to the girls' parents for the mayor's daughter to join them at the river. Finally, he agreed. The mother took to her bed with a sick headache when she thought of her lovely daughter removing her clothes in front of the uncouth spawn of her husband's constituents: rough farmers and their sun-darkened wives.

Kiki removed all her clothes with glee as soon as the group arrived at the river. She ran to the water tossing lace, satin, and silk over her head. She behaved like a bird whose cage door had been opened for the first time. The girls giggled at the sight of the freckles on her shoulders, her little pink nipples, like rosebuds, her golden hair. But since she was the mayor's daughter, they dared not get too close. They acted more like her attendants than her friends. Kiki would have ended up alone again if it had not been for Marina.

Marina was awestruck by the exuberant Kiki; and Kiki was drawn to the quiet girl who watched the others at play with such yearning. Soon the two girls were inseparable. Marina would take Kiki's wet hair, like molten gold, into her brown hands and weave it into two perfect plaits which she would pin to the girl's head like a crown. It was fascinating to watch how the two came together word-lessly, like partners in a *pas de deux*.

It was an idyllic time, until one afternoon Marina and Kiki did not return to the river from an excursion into the woods where they had ostensibly gone to gather flowers. Mamá and her friends searched for them until nearly dark, but did not find them. The mayor went in person to notify Marina's mother of the situation. What he found was a woman who had fallen permanently into silence: secluded in a secret place of shadows where she wished to remain.

It was the events of one night long ago that had made her aban- 27 don the world.

Marina's mother had lost her young husband and delivered her 28 child prematurely on the same night. The news that her man had been drowned in a fishing accident had brought on an agonizing labor. She had had a son, a tiny little boy, perfect in his parts, but sickly. The new mother, weakened in body and mind by so much pain, had decided that she preferred a daughter for company. Hysterically, she had begged the anxious midwife to keep her secret. And as soon as she was able to walk to church, she had the child dressed in a flowing gown of lace and had her christened Marina. Living the life a recluse, to which she was entitled as a widow, and attended by her loyal nurse, and later, by her quiet obedient Marina, the woman had slipped easily out of reality.

By the time Marina was old enough to discover the difference 29 between her body and the bodies of her girlfriends, her mother had forgotten all about having borne a son. In fact, the poor soul would have been horrified to discover a man under her roof. And so Marina kept up appearances, waiting out her body's dictates year by year. The summer that Kiki joined the bathers at the río, Marina had made up her mind to run away from home. She had been in torment until the blonde girl had appeared like an angel, bringing Marina the balm of her presence and the soothing touch of her hands.

The mayor found the woman sitting calmly in a rocking chair. 30 She looked like a wax figure dressed in widow's weeds. Only her elegant hands moved as she crocheted a collar for a little girl's dress. And although she smiled deferentially at the men speaking loudly in her parlor, she remained silent. Silence was the place she had inhabited for years, and no one could draw her out now.

Furious, the mayor threatened to have her arrested. Finally it 31 was the old nurse who confessed the whole sad tale—to the horror of the mayor and his men. She handed him an envelope with *Papá y Mamá* written on its face in Kiki's hand. In a last show of control, the mayor took the sealed letter home to read in the privacy of the family mansion where his wife was waiting, still under the impression that the two girls had been kidnapped for political reasons.

Kiki's letter explained briefly that she and *Marino* had eloped. 32 They had fallen in love and nothing and no one could change their minds about getting married. She had sold her pearl necklace—the family heirloom given to her by her parents to wear at her quinceañera, and they were using the money for passage on the next steamship out of San Juan to New York.

The mayor did not finish his term in office. He and his wife, now ₃₃ a recluse, exiled themselves to Spain.

"And Marina and Kiki?" I had asked Mamá, eager for more ₃₄ details about Kiki and Marino. "What happened to them?"

"What happens to *any* married couple?" Mamá had replied, ₃₅ putting an end to her story. "They had several children, they worked, they got old . . ." She chuckled gently at my naiveté.

On our way back through town from our walk, Mother and I ₃₆ again saw Marino with his pretty granddaughter. This time he was lifting her to smell a white rose that grew from a vine entangled on a tree branch. The child brought the flower carefully to her nose and smelled it. Then the old man placed the child gently back on the ground and they continued their promenade, stopping to examine anything that caught the child's eye.

"Do you think he made a good husband?" I asked my mother. ₃₇

"He would know what it takes to make a woman happy," she ₃₈ said as she turned to face me, and winked in camaraderie.

As I watched the gentle old man and the little girl, I imagined ₃₉ Marina sitting alone on the banks of a river, his heart breaking with pain and wild yearnings, listening to the girls asking questions he could have answered; remaining silent; learning patience, until love would give him the right to reclaim his original body and destiny. Yet he would never forget the lessons she learned at the río—or how to handle fragile things. I looked at my mother and she smiled at me; we now had a new place to begin our search for the meaning of the word *woman*.

THE UNAUTHORIZED AUTOBIOGRAPHY OF ME

Sherman J. Alexie Jr.

Late summer night on the Spokane Indian Reservation. Ten 1
Indians are playing basketball on a court barely illuminated by the
streetlight above them. They will play until the brown, leather ball is
invisible in the dark. They will play until an errant pass jams a finger,
knocks a pair of glasses off a face, smashes a nose and draws blood.
They will play until the ball bounces off the court and disappears into
the shadows.

Sometimes, I think this is all you need to know about Native 2
American literature.

Thesis: I have never met a Native American. Thesis reiterated: I have 3
met thousands of Indians.

PEN American panel in Manhattan, November 1994, on Indian 4
Literature. N. Scott Momaday, James Welch, Gloria Miguel, Joy
Harjo, and myself. Two or three hundred people in the audience.
Mostly non-Indians; an Indian or three. Questions and answers.

"Why do you insist on calling yourselves Indian?" asked a white 5
woman in a nice hat. "It's so demeaning."

"Listen," I said. "The word belongs to us now. We are Indians. 6
That has nothing to do with Indians from India. We are not American
Indians. We are Indians, pronounced In-din. It belongs to us. We own
it and we're not going to give it back."

So much has been taken from us that we hold on to the smallest 7
things with all the strength we have left.

Winter on the Spokane Indian Reservation, 1976. My two cousins, S 8
and G, have enough money for gloves. They buy them at Irene's
Grocery Store. Irene is a white woman who has lived on our reservation since the beginning of time. I have no money for gloves. My
hands are bare.

We build snow fortresses on the football field. Since we are 9
Indian boys playing, there must be a war. We stockpile snowballs. S
and G build their fortress on the fifty-yard line. I build mine on the
thirty-yard line. We begin our little war. My hands are bare.

My cousins are good warriors. They throw snowballs with preci- 10
sion. I am bombarded, under siege, defeated quickly. My cousins
bury me in the snow. My grave is shallow. If my cousins knew how
to dance, they might have danced on my grave. But they know how
to laugh, so they laugh. They are my cousins, meaning we are related
in the Indian way. My father drank beers with their father for most of
two decades, and that is enough to make us relatives. Indians gather
relatives like firewood, protection against the cold. I am buried in the
snow, cold, without protection. My hands are bare.

After a short celebration, my cousins exhume me. I am too cold 11
to fight. Shivering, I walk for home, anxious for warmth. I know my
mother is home. She is probably sewing a quilt. She is always sewing
quilts. If she sells a quilt, we have dinner. If she fails to sell a quilt, we
go hungry. My mother has never failed to sell a quilt. But the threat
of hunger is always there.

When I step into the house, my mother is sewing yet another 12
quilt. She is singing a song under her breath. You might assume she
is singing a highly traditional Spokane Indian song. She is singing
Donna Fargo's "The Happiest Girl in the Whole USA." Improbably,
this is a highly traditional Spokane Indian song. The living room is
dark in the late afternoon. The house is cold. My mother is wearing
her coat and shoes.

"Why don't you turn up the heat?" I ask my mother.   13

"No electricity," she says.   14

"Power went out?" I ask.   15

"Didn't pay the bill," she says.   16

I am colder. I inhale, exhale, my breath visible inside the house. I 17
can hear a car sliding on the icy road outside. My mother is making
a quilt. This quilt will pay for the electricity. Her fingers are stiff and
painful from the cold. She is sewing as fast as she can.

On the jukebox in the bar: Hank Williams, Patsy Cline, Johnny Cash, 18
Charlie Rich, Freddy Fender, Donna Fargo.

On the radio in the car: Creedence Clearwater Revival, Three 19
Dog Night, Blood, Sweat and Tears, Janis Joplin, early Stones, earlier
Beatles.

On the stereo in the house: Glen Campbell, Roy Orbison, Johnny 20
Horton, Loretta Lynn, "The Ballad of the Green Beret."

The fourth-grade music teacher, Mr. Manley, set a row of musical 21
instruments in front of us. From left to right, a flute, clarinet, French

horn, trombone, trumpet, tuba, drum. We had our first chance to play that kind of music.

"Now," he explained, "I want all of you to line up behind the 22 instrument you want to learn how to play."

Dawn, Loretta, and Karen lined up behind the flute. Melissa and 23 Michelle behind the clarinet. Lori and Willette behind the French horn. All ten Indian boys lined up behind the drum.

My sister, Mary, was beautiful. She was fourteen years older than me. 24 She wore short skirts and nylons because she was supposed to wear short skirts and nylons. It was expected. Her black hair combed long and straight. 1970. Often, she sat in her favorite chair, the fake leather lounger we rescued from the dump. Holding a hand mirror, she combed her hair, applied her makeup. Much lipstick and eyeshadow, no foundation. She was always leaving the house. I do not remember where she went. I do remember sitting at her feet, rubbing my cheek against her nyloned calf, while she waited for her ride.

She died in an early morning fire in Montana in 1981. At the time, 25 I was sleeping at a friend's house in Washington. I was not dreaming of my sister.

"Sherman," asks the critic, "how does your work apply to the oral 26 tradition?"

"Well," I say, as I hold my latest book close to me, "it doesn't 27 apply at all because I type this. And I'm really, really quiet when I'm typing it."

Summer 1977. Steve and I want to attend the KISS concert in 28 Spokane. KISS is very popular on my reservation. Gene Simmons, the bass player. Paul Stanley, lead singer and rhythm guitarist. Ace Frehley, lead guitar. Peter Criss, drummer. All four hide their faces behind elaborate makeup. Simmons the devil, Stanley the lover, Frehley the space man, Criss the cat.

The songs: "Do You Love Me," "Calling Dr. Love," "Love Gun," 29 "Makin' Love," "C'mon and Love Me."

Steve and I are too young to go on our own. His uncle and aunt, 30 born-again Christians, decide to chaperon us. Inside the Spokane Coliseum, the four of us find seats far from the stage and the enormous speakers. Uncle and Aunt wanted to avoid the bulk of the crowd, but have landed us in the unofficial pot smoking section. We are over-whelmed by the sweet smoke. Steve and I cover our mouths and noses with Styrofoam cups and try to breathe normally.

KISS opens their show with staged explosions, flashing red ₃₁
lights, a prolonged guitar solo by Frehley. Simmons spits fire. The
crowd rushes the stage. All the pot smokers in our section hold
lighters, tiny flames flickering, high above their heads. The songs are
so familiar. We know all the words. The audience sings along.

The songs: "Let Me Go, Rock 'n Roll," "Detroit Rock City," "Rock ₃₂
and Roll All Nite."

The decibel level is tremendous. Steve and I can feel the sound ₃₃
waves crashing against the Styrofoam cups we hold over our faces.
Aunt and Uncle are panicked, finally assured that the devil plays a
mean guitar. This is too much for them. It is too much for Steve and
me, but we pretend to be disappointed when Aunt and Uncle drag
us out of the coliseum.

During the drive home, Aunt and Uncle play Christian music on ₃₄
the radio. Loudly and badly, they sing along. Steve and I are in the
back of the Pacer, looking up through the strangely curved rear window. There is a meteor shower, the largest in a decade. Steve and I
smell like pot smoke. We smile at this. Our ears ring. We make wishes
on the shooting stars, though both of us know that a shooting star is
not a star. It's just a sliver of stone.

I made a very conscious decision to marry an Indian woman, who ₃₅
made a very conscious decision to marry me.

Our hope: to give birth to and raise Indian children who love ₃₆
themselves. That is the most revolutionary act possible.

1982. I am the only Indian student at Reardan High, an all-white ₃₇
school in a small farm town just outside my reservation. I am in the
pizza parlor, sharing a deluxe with my white friends. We are talking
and laughing. A drunk Indian walks into the parlor. He staggers to
the counter and orders a beer. The waiter ignores him. Our table is
silent.

At our table, S is shaking her head. She leans toward the table as ₃₈
if to share a secret. We all lean toward her.

"Man," she says, "I hate Indians." ₃₉

I am curious about the Indian writers who identify themselves as ₄₀
mixed-blood. It must be difficult for them, trying to decide into which
container they should place their nouns and verbs. Yet, it must be good
to be invisible, as a blond, Aryan-featured Jew might have known in
Germany during World War II. Then again, I think of the horror stories
that a pale Jew might tell about his life during the Holocaust.

An Incomplete List of People Whom I Wish Were Indian

1. Martin Luther King Jr.
2. Robert Johnson
3. Meryl Streep
4. Helen Keller
5. Walt Whitman
6. Emily Dickinson
7. Superman
8. Adam
9. Eve
10. Muhammad Ali
11. Billie Jean King
12. John Lennon
13. Jimmy Carter
14. Rosa Parks
15. Shakespeare
16. John Steinbeck
17. Billy the Kid
18. Voltaire
19. Harriet Tubman
20. Flannery O'Connor
21. Pablo Neruda
22. Amelia Earhart
23. Sappho
24. Mary Magdalene
25. Robert DeNiro
26. Susan B. Anthony
27. Kareem Abdul-Jabbar
28. Wilma Rudolph
29. Isadora Duncan
30. Bruce Springsteen
31. Dian Fossey
32. Patsy Cline
33. Jesus Christ

Summer 1995. Seattle, Washington. I am idling at a red light [41] when a car filled with white boys pulls up beside me. The white boy in the front passenger seat leans out his window.

"I hate you Indian motherfuckers," he screams. [42]

I quietly wait for the green light. [43]

1978. David, Randy, Steve, and I decide to form a reservation doo- 44
wop group, like the Temptations. During recess, we practice behind
the old tribal school. Steve, a falsetto, is the best singer. I am the worst
singer, but have the deepest voice, and am therefore an asset.

"What songs do you want to sing?" asks David. 45

"'Tracks of My Tears,'" says Steve, who always decides these 46
kind of things.

We sing, desperately trying to remember the lyrics to that song. 47
We try to remember other songs. We remember the chorus to most,
the first verse of a few, and only one in its entirety. For some
unknown reason, we all know the lyrics of "Monster Mash," a nov-
elty hit from the fifties. However, I'm the only one who can manage
to sing with the pseudo-Transylvanian accent that "Monster Mash"
requires. This dubious skill makes me the lead singer, despite Steve's
protests.

"We need a name for our group," says Randy. 48

"How about The Warriors?" I ask. 49

Everybody agrees. We watch westerns. 50

We sing "Monster Mash" over and over. We want to be famous. 51
We want all the little Indian girls to shout our names. Finally, after
days of practice, we are ready for our debut. Walking in a row like
soldiers, the four of us parade around the playground. We sing
"Monster Mash." I am in front, followed by Steve, David, then
Randy, who is the shortest, but the toughest fighter our reservation
has ever known. We sing. We are The Warriors. All the other Indian
boys and girls line up behind us as we march. We are heroes. We are
loved. I sing with everything I have inside of me: pain, happiness,
anger, depression, heart, soul, small intestine. I sing and am
rewarded with people who listen.

This is why I am a poet. 52

I remember watching Richard Nixon, during the whole Watergate 53
affair, as he held a press conference and told the entire world that he
was not a liar.

For the first time, I understood that storytellers could be bad 54
people.

Poetry = Anger • Imagination

Every time I venture into the bookstore, I find another book about 55
Indians. There are hundreds of books about Indians published every

year, yet so few are written by Indians. I gather all the books written about Indians. I discover:

1. A book written by a person who identifies herself as mixed-blood will sell more copies than a book written by a person who identifies herself as strictly Indian.
2. A book written by a non-Indian will sell more copies than a book written by a mixed-blood or Indian writer.
3. A book about Indian life in the pre-twentieth century, whether written by a non-Indian, mixed-blood, or Indian, will sell more copies than a book about twentieth-century Indian life.
4. If you are a non-Indian writing about Indians, it is almost guaranteed that Tony Hillerman will write something positive about you.
5. Reservation Indian writers are rarely published in any form.
6. Every Indian woman writer will be compared with Louise Erdrich. Every Indian man writer will be compared with Michael Dorris.
7. A very small percentage of the readers of Indian literature have heard of Simon J. Ortiz. This is a crime.
8. Books about the Sioux sell more copies than all of the books written about other tribes combined.
9. Mixed-blood writers often write about any tribe that interests them, whether or not the writer is descended from that tribe.
10. Most of the writers who use obviously Indian names, such as Eagle Woman and Pretty Shield, are usually non-Indian.
11. Non-Indian writers usually say "Great Spirit," "Mother Earth," "Two-Legged, Four-Legged, and Winged." Mixed-blood writers usually say "Creator," "Mother Earth," "Two-Legged, Four-Legged, and Winged." Indian writers usually say "God," "Earth," "Human Being, Dog, and Bird."
12. If an Indian book contains no dogs, then the book is written by a non-Indian or mixed-blood writer.
13. If there are winged animals who aren't supposed to have wings on the cover of the book, then it is written by a non-Indian.
14. Successful non-Indian writers are thought to be learned experts on Indian life. Successful mixed-blood writers are thought to be wonderful translators of Indian life. Successful Indian writers are thought to be traditional storytellers of Indian life.
15. Very few Indian and mixed-blood writers speak their tribal languages. Even fewer non-Indian writers speak their tribal languages.

16. Mixed-bloods often write exclusively about Indians, even if they grew up in non-Indian communities.
17. Indians often write exclusively about reservation life, even if they never lived on a reservation.
18. Non-Indian writers always write about reservation life.
19. Nobody has written the great urban Indian novel yet.
20. Most non-Indians who write about Indians are fiction writers. They write fiction about Indians because it sells.

Have you stood in a crowded room where nobody looks like ⁵⁶ you? If you are white, have you stood in a room full of black people? Are you an Irish man who has strolled through the streets of Compton? If you are black, have you stood in a room full of white people? Are you an African man who has been playing the back nine at the local country club? If you are a woman, have you stood in a room full of men? Are you Sandra Day O'Connor or Ruth Ginsburg?

Since I left the reservation, almost every room I enter is filled ⁵⁷ with people who do not look like me. There are only two million Indians in this country. We could all fit into one medium-sized city. We should look into it.

Often, I am most alone in bookstores where I am reading from ⁵⁸ my work. I look up from the page at a sea of white faces. This is frightening.

There was an apple tree outside my grandmother's house on the ⁵⁹ reservation. The apples were green; my grandmother's house was green. This was the game. My siblings and I would try to sneak apples from the tree. Sometimes, our friends would join our raiding expeditions. My grandmother believed green apples were poison and was simply trying to protect us from sickness. There is nothing biblical about this story.

The game had rules. We always had to raid the tree during day- ⁶⁰ light. My grandmother had bad eyes and it would have been unfair to challenge her during the dark. We all had to approach the tree at the same time. Arnold, my older brother, Kim and Arlene, my younger twin sisters. We had to climb the tree to steal apples, ignoring the fruit that hung low to the ground.

Arnold, of course, was the best apple thief on the reservation. He ⁶¹ was chubby but quick. He was fearless in the tree, climbing to the top for the plumpest apples. He'd hang from a branch with one arm, reach for apples with the other, and fill his pockets with his booty. I loved him like crazy. My sisters were more conservative. They often grabbed one apple and ate it quickly while they sat on a sturdy branch. I always wanted the green apples that contained a hint of red. While we were busy raiding the tree, we'd also keep an eye on my grandmother's house. She was a big woman, nearly six feet tall. At the age of seventy, she could still outrun any ten-year-old.

Arnold, of course, was always the first kid out of the tree. He'd 62 hang from a branch, drop to the ground, and scream loudly, announcing our presence to our grandmother. He'd run away, leaving my sisters and me stuck in the tree. We'd scramble to the ground and try to escape. If our grandmother said our name, we were automatically captured.

"Junior," she'd shout and I'd freeze. It was the rule. A dozen 63 Indian kids were sometimes in that tree, scattering in random directions when our grandmother burst out of the house. If our grandmother remembered your name, you were a prisoner of war. And, believe me, no matter how many kids were running away, my grandmother always remembered my name.

"Junior," she'd shout and I would close my eyes in disgust. 64 Captured again! I'd wait as she walked up to me. She'd hold out her hand and I'd give her any stolen apples. Then she'd smack me gently on the top of my head. I was free to run then, pretending she'd never caught me in the first place. I'd try to catch up with my siblings and friends. I would shout their names as I ran through the trees surrounding my grandmother's house.

My grandmother died when I was fourteen years old. I miss her. 65 I miss everybody.

So many people claim to be Indian, speaking of an Indian grand- 66 mother, a warrior grandfather. Let's say the United States government announced that every Indian had to return to their reservation. How many people would shove their Indian ancestor back into the closet?

My mother still makes quilts. My wife and I sleep beneath one. 67 My brother works for our tribal casino. One sister works for our bingo hall, while the other works in the tribal finance department. Our adopted little brother, James, who is actually our second cousin, is a freshman at Reardan High School. He can run the mile in five minutes.

My father used to leave us for weeks at a time to drink with his 68 friends and cousins. I missed him so much I'd cry myself sick. Every time he left, I ended up in the emergency room. But I always got well and he always came back. He'd walk in the door without warning. We'd forgive him.

I could always tell when he was going to leave. He would be tense, quiet, unable to concentrate. He'd flip through magazines and television channels. He'd open the refrigerator door, study its contents, shut the door, and walk away. Five minutes later, he'd be back at the fridge, rearranging items on the shelves. I would follow him from place to place, trying to prevent his escape. 69

Once, he went into the bathroom, which had no windows, while I sat outside the only door and waited for him. I could not hear him inside. I knocked on the thin wood. I was five years old. 70

"Are you there?" I asked. "Are you still there?" 71

Years later, I am giving a reading at a bookstore in Spokane, Washington. There is a large crowd. I read a story about an Indian father who leaves his family for good. He moves to a city a thousand miles away. Then he dies. It is a sad story. When I finish, a woman in the front row breaks into tears. 72

"What's wrong?" I ask her. 73

"I'm so sorry about your father," she says. 74

"Thank you," I say. "But that's my father sitting right next to you." 75

THE MEN WE CARRY IN OUR MINDS

Scott Russell Sanders

When I was a boy, the men I knew labored with their bodies. 1
They were marginal farmers, just scraping by, or welders, steelwork-
ers, carpenters; they swept floors, dug ditches, mined coal, or drove
trucks, their forearms ropy with muscle; they trained horses, stoked
furnaces, built tires, stood on assembly lines wrestling parts onto cars
and refrigerators. They got up before light, worked all day long
whatever the weather, and when they came home at night they
looked as though somebody had been whipping them. In the
evenings and on weekends they worked on their own places, tilling
gardens that were lumpy with clay, fixing broken-down cars, ham-
mering on houses that were always too drafty, too leaky, too small.

The bodies of the men I knew were twisted and maimed in ways 2
visible and invisible. The nails of their hands were black and split, the
hands tattooed with scars. Some had lost fingers. Heavy lifting had
given many of them finicky backs and guts weak from hernias.
Racing against conveyor belts had given them ulcers. Their ankles
and knees ached from years of standing on concrete. Anyone who
had worked for long around machines was hard of hearing. They
squinted, and the skin of their faces was creased like the leather of
old work gloves. There were times, studying them, when I dreaded
growing up. Most of them coughed, from dust or cigarettes, and
most of them drank cheap wine or whiskey, so their eyes looked
bloodshot and bruised. The fathers of my friends always seemed
older than the mothers. Men wore out sooner. Only women lived into
old age.

As a boy I also knew another sort of men, who did not sweat and 3
break down like mules. They were soldiers, and so far as I could tell
they scarcely worked at all. During my early school years we lived on
a military base, an arsenal in Ohio, and every day I saw GIs in the
guardshacks, on the stoops of barracks, at the wheels of olive drab
Chevrolets. The chief fact of their lives was boredom. Long after I left
the Arsenal I came to recognize the sour smell the soldiers gave off as
that of souls in limbo. They were all waiting—for wars, for transfers,
for leaves, for promotions, for the end of their hitch—like so many
braves waiting for the hunt to begin. Unlike the warriors of older
tribes, however, they would have no say about when the battle
would start or how it would be waged. Their waiting was broken

only when they practiced for war. They fired guns at targets, drove tanks across the churned-up fields of the military reservation, set off bombs in the wrecks of old fighter planes. I knew this was all play. But I also felt certain that when the hour for killing arrived, they would kill. When the real shooting started, many of them would die. This was what soldiers were *for*, just as a hammer was for driving nails.

Warriors and toilers: those seemed, in my boyhood vision, to be the 4 chief destinies for men. They weren't the only destinies, as I learned from having a few male teachers, from reading books, and from watching television. But the men on television—the politicians, the astronauts, the generals, the savvy lawyers, the philosophical doctors, the bosses who gave orders to both soldiers and laborers— seemed as removed and unreal to me as the figures in tapestries. I could no more imagine growing up to become one of these cool, potent creatures than I could imagine becoming a prince.

A nearer and more hopeful example was that of my father, who 5 had escaped from a red-dirt farm to a tire factory, and from the assembly line to the front office. Eventually he dressed in a white shirt and tie. He carried himself as if he had been born to work with his mind. But his body, remembering the earlier years of slogging work, began to give out on him in his fifties, and it quit on him entirely before he turned sixty-five. Even such a partial escape from man's fate as he had accomplished did not seem possible for most of the boys I knew. They joined the Army, stood in line for jobs in the smoky plants, helped build highways. They were bound to work as their fathers had worked, killing themselves or preparing to kill others.

A scholarship enabled me not only to attend college, a rare 6 enough feat in my circle, but even to study in a university meant for the children of the rich. Here I met for the first time young men who had assumed from birth that they would lead lives of comfort and power. And for the first time I met women who told me that men were guilty of having kept all the joys and privileges of the earth for themselves. I was baffled. What privileges? What joys? I thought about the maimed, dismal lives of most of the men back home. What had they stolen from their wives and daughters? The right to go five days a week, twelve months a year, for thirty or forty years to a steel mill or a coal mine? The right to drop bombs and die in war? The right to feel every leak in the roof, every gap in the fence, every cough in the engine, as a wound they must mend? The right to feel, when the lay-off comes or the plant shuts down, not only afraid but ashamed?

I was slow to understand the deep grievances of women. This 7 was because, as a boy, I had envied them. Before college, the only people I had ever known who were interested in art or music or literature, the only ones who read books, the only ones who ever seemed to enjoy a sense of ease and grace were the mothers and daughters. Like the menfolk, they fretted about money, they scrimped and made-do. But, when the pay stopped coming in, they were not the ones who had failed. Nor did they have to go to war, and that seemed to me a blessed fact. By comparison with the narrow, ironclad days of fathers, there was an expansiveness, I thought, in the days of mothers. They went to see neighbors, to shop in town, to run errands at school, at the library, at church. No doubt, had I looked harder at their lives, I would have envied them less. It was not my fate to become a woman, so it was easier for me to see the graces. Few of them held jobs outside the home, and those who did filled thankless roles as clerks and waitresses. I didn't see, then, what a prison a house could be, since houses seemed to me brighter, handsomer places than any factory. I did not realize—because such things were never spoken of—how often women suffered from men's bullying. I did learn about the wretchedness of abandoned wives, single mothers, widows; but I also learned about the wretchedness of lone men. Even then I could see how exhausting it was for a mother to cater all day to the needs of young children. But if I had been asked, as a boy, to choose between tending a baby and tending a machine, I think I would have chosen the baby. (Having now tended both, I know I would choose the baby.)

So I was baffled when the women at college accused me and my 8 sex of having cornered the world's pleasures. I think something like my bafflement has been felt by other boys (and by girls as well) who grew up in dirt-poor farm country, in mining country, in black ghettos, in Hispanic barrios, in the shadows of factories, in Third World nations—any place where the fate of men is as grim and bleak as the fate of women. Toilers and warriors. I realize now how ancient these identities are, how deep the tug they exert on men, the undertow of a thousand generations. The miseries I saw, as a boy, in the lives of nearly all men I continue to see in the lives of many—the body-breaking toil, the tedium, the call to be tough, the humiliating powerlessness, the battle for a living and for territory.

When the women I met at college thought about the joys and 9 privileges of men, they did not carry in their minds the sort of men I had known in my childhood. They thought of their fathers, who were bankers, physicians, architects, stockbrokers, the big wheels of the big cities. These fathers rode the train to work or drove cars that cost more than any of my childhood houses. They were attended from morning to night by female helpers, wives and nurses and secretaries. They were never laid off, never short of cash at month's end, never lined up for welfare. These fathers made decisions that mattered. They ran the world.

The daughters of such men wanted to share in this power, this 10 glory. So did I. They yearned for a say over their future, for jobs worthy of their abilities, for the right to live at peace, unmolested, whole. Yes, I thought, yes yes. The difference between me and these daughters was that they saw me, because of my sex, as destined from birth to become like their fathers, and therefore as an enemy to their desires. But I knew better. I wasn't an enemy, in fact or in feeling. I was an ally. If I had known, then, how to tell them so, would they have believed me? Would they now?

3

INVESTIGATING

READING STATISTICAL TEA LEAVES

Karen W. Arenson

Harold Hodgkinson likes to say that "demography is destiny." [1] As a demographer focused on education, he has looked at how births, ethnic backgrounds, family income and other factors shape education. He is convinced that careful scrutiny of such data can lead to better education policy. A former dean at Simmons and Bard colleges, Dr. Hodgkinson led the National Institute of Education under President Gerald R. Ford. Since 1987, he has directed the Center for Demographic Policy at the Institute for Educational Leadership in Washington.

What is the most important demographic trend affecting higher education? The No. 1 demographic change is probably the increase in ethnic diversity in America. If you look 20 years out, 63 percent of the new population growth in the United States will be Hispanic and Asian. And virtually all of the diversity in America is concentrated in 10 states. Hispanics are now the largest minority group in the United States, and 34 percent of them live in California, 19 percent in Texas, 10 percent in New York and 7 percent in Florida. All of the other states are under 5 percent. Of the Asian population in America, nearly half live in three metropolitan areas, San Francisco, Los Angeles and New York. And 75 percent of the black population is in the Southeast and the Mississippi Delta.

What does that mean for colleges? There is a move afoot to have every college be a mirror of the national population distribution. Given that 80 percent of kids going to college do so in their own state, looking like the country as a whole becomes a challenge in a state where minorities are 10 percent of the population. It also raises the issue of whether you should have the same proportion of minority faculty. The recruitment of minority faculty becomes a real crisis, because graduate schools are not turning out that many minority Ph.D.'s. One area where there will be a real problem is in developing new teachers. There has been a fairly pervasive decline in the number of blacks and Hispanics majoring in education—a decline of about 30 percent.

You say you like demographics because population trends are predictable. Have there been any surprises in the last 20 years? There was only one surprise: the percentage of children living below the poverty line.

The strong economy pushed it down somewhat in recent years, but for decades the number was about 20 percent of American children. Any lessons there for colleges and universities? For the lowest 20 percent, the amount of household income required to send children to college has increased, while their income has not increased at all. Tuition as a proportion of income has risen. But as we look at programs to help the poor, we have to remember that they are not all minorities. We tend to associate poverty mostly with minorities. But the largest number of poor children are white. Of the 14 million poor children in 1999, 8.9 million were white, 4 million were black and 3.9 million were Hispanic. But the children in poverty represented 16 percent of all white children, 37 percent of all black children and 36 percent of Hispanic children.

What are some of the other demographic trends? People are moving much more frequently. About 43 million Americans move every year. That means people are changing jobs, and employers need to know who they are and what they can do. So they need a piece of paper—a college diploma or a certificate stating their skills. That is putting pressure on universities and colleges for those pieces of paper to mean the same thing. But there is almost no way you can guarantee that they do. It will only be a matter of time before states require tests to show what students have learned in college. But that would be terrible.

Did anyone predict there would be so many adult students? Nobody in 1980 assumed that the number of adults going to college would be so high today. Of the 15 million students in college, almost half of them are adults with kids and jobs. The Joe College stereotype—the 18- to 22-year-old full-time student in residence on a campus—accounts for only 20 percent of the 15 million students.

Has the increase in older students run its course, or do you think it will continue? I think it will continue. A lot of people are beginning to come back to higher education for a capstone experience in their 40's, 50's and 60's. Not for a better job, but for a vindication of their life. I was speaking at a commencement a few months ago and an older man walked across the stage to receive his doctoral degree. Someone shouted out, "Way to go, grandpa." I just love it. There is no reason to think that higher education was designed solely for the post-pubescent adolescent.

What does that mean for colleges faced with serving such students? Older students have different needs. A whole lot of 30- and 40-year-olds have been out of education a long time. They may have a lot of innate smarts, but they don't remember the quadratic equation. So a lot of remedial education is to get 40-year-olds to remember how to write a good theme, and that is fine.

Many of the immigrants who come to the United States count on higher education to help them make it. How well does it work for them? American higher education performs a unique function. No other country takes such a diverse group of people and turns them into the middle class. In the 1900's, it worked for Italians, Germans, French and English-speaking immigrants. Now it is working for Koreans and the Hmong. It is even working for the black population that is already here. Twenty percent of black households now have a higher income than the average for white households.

That's never been true before. The mobility machine is clicking along like it should. We're very cynical, especially about our education system. But we need some appreciation for the kind of miracle we accomplish that doesn't happen in other countries—it's all due to our system of education.

So is college really available to all? The percentage of college students who are minorities is virtually the same in every state as the percentage of high school students who are minorities. In California, for example, 54 percent of high school graduates are minorities, while 53 percent of college students are minorities. In Minnesota, 10 percent of high school graduates are minorities, while 9 percent of college students are minorities.

If you had a billion dollars to invest in education, how would you spend it? I would spend most of it on the years before college, not on colleges. Money spent on Head Start and Trio and other precollege programs saves lots of money later on. To remediate someone at age 20 when their last 14 years were misused is really a chore. It can be done. But it is not efficient. College is really the icing on the cake.

WHY THEY EXCEL

Fox Butterfield

Kim-Chi Trinh was just 9 in Vietnam when her father used his 1
savings to buy a passage for her on a fishing boat. It was a costly and
risky sacrifice for the family, placing Kim-Chi on the small boat,
among strangers, in hopes she would eventually reach the United
States, where she would get a good education and enjoy a better life.
Before the boat reached safety in Malaysia, the supply of food and
water ran out.

Still alone, Kim-Chi made it to the United States, coping with a 2
succession of three foster families. But when she graduated from San
Diego's Patrick Henry High School in 1988, she had a straight-A average and scholarship offers from Stanford and Cornell universities.

"I have to do well—it's not even a question," said the diminutive 3
19-year-old, now a sophomore at Cornell. "I owe it to my parents in
Vietnam."

Kim-Chi is part of a tidal wave of bright, highly motivated 4
Asian-Americans who are suddenly surging into our best colleges.
Although Asian-Americans make up only 2.4 percent of the nation's
population, they constitute 17.1 percent of the undergraduates at
Harvard, 18 percent at the Massachusetts Institute of Technology and
27.3 percent at the University of California at Berkeley.

With Asians being the fastest-growing ethnic group in the 5
country—two out of five immigrants are now Asian—these figures
will increase. At the University of California at Irvine, a staggering
35.1 percent of the undergraduates are Asian-American, but the proportion in the freshman class is even higher: 41 percent.

Why are the Asian-Americans doing so well? Are they grinds, as 6
some stereotypes suggest? Do they have higher IQs? Or are they
actually teaching the rest of us a lesson about values we have long
treasured but may have misplaced—like hard work, the family and
education?

Not all Asians are doing equally well. Poorly educated 7
Cambodian and Hmong refugee youngsters need special help. And
Asian-Americans resent being labeled a "model minority," feeling
that is just another form of prejudice by white Americans, an ironic
reversal of the discriminatory laws that excluded most Asian immi-
gration to America until 1965.

But the academic success of many Asian-Americans has 8 prompted growing concern among educators, parents and other students. Some universities have what look like unofficial quotas, much as Ivy League colleges did against Jews in the 1920s and '30s. Berkeley Chancellor Ira Heyman apologized last spring for an admissions policy that, he said, had "a disproportionately negative impact on Asian-Americans."

I have wondered about the reason for the Asians' success since I 9 was a fledgling journalist on Taiwan in 1969. That year, a team of boys from a poor, isolated mountain village on Taiwan won the annual Little League World Series at Williamsport, Pa. Their victory was totally unexpected. At the time, baseball was a largely unknown sport on Taiwan, and the boys had learned to play with bamboo sticks for bats and rocks for balls. But since then, teams from Taiwan, Japan or South Korea have won the Little League championship in 16 out of the 21 years. How could, these Asian boys beat us at our own game?

Fortunately, the young Asians' achievements have led to a series 10 of intriguing studies. "There is something going on here that we as Americans need to understand," said Sanford M. Dornbusch, a professor of sociology at Stanford. Dornbusch, in surveys of 7000 students in six San Francisco-area high schools, found that Asian-Americans consistently get better grades than any other group of students, regardless of their parents' level of education or their families' social and economic status, the usual predictors of success. In fact, those in homes where English is spoken often, or whose families have lived longer in the United States, do slightly less well.

"We used to talk about the American melting pot as an advan- 11 tage," Dornbusch said. "But the sad fact is that it has become a melting pot with low standards."

Other studies have shown similar results. Perhaps the most 12 disturbing have come in a series of studies by a University of Michigan psychologist, Harold W. Stevenson, who has compared more than 7000 students in kindergarten, first grade, third grade and fifth grade in Chicago and Minneapolis with counterparts in Beijing; Sendai, Japan; and Taipei, Taiwan. On a battery of math tests, the Americans did worst at all grade levels.

Stevenson found no differences in IQ. But if the differences in 13 performance are showing up in kindergarten, it suggests something is happening in the family, even before the children get to school.

It is here that the various studies converge: Asian parents are able 14 to instill more motivation in their children. "My bottom line is, Asian kids work hard," said Professor Dornbusch.

In his survey of San Francisco-area high schools, for example, he 15
reported that Asian-Americans do an average of 7.03 hours of homework a week. Non-Hispanic whites average 6.12 hours, blacks 4.23
hours and Hispanics 3.98 hours. Asians also score highest on a series
of other measures of effort, such as fewer class cuts and paying more
attention to the teacher.

Don Lee, 20, is a junior at Berkeley. His parents immigrated to 16
Torrance, Calif., from South Korea when he was 5, so he could get a
better education. Lee said his father would warn him about the danger of wasting time at high school dances or football games.
"Instead," he added, "for fun on weekends, my friends and I would
go to the town library to study."

The real question, then, is how do Asian parents imbue their off- 17
spring with this kind of motivation? Stevenson's study suggests a
critical answer. When the Asian parents were asked why they think
their children do well, they most often said "hard work." By contrast,
American parents said "talent."

"From what I can see," said Stevenson, "we've lost our belief in 18
the Horatio Alger myth that anyone can get ahead in life through
pluck and hard work. Instead, Americans now believe that some kids
have it and some don't, so we begin dividing up classes into fast
learners and slow learners, where the Chinese and Japanese believe
all children can learn from the same curriculum."

The Asians' belief in hard work also springs from their common 19
heritage of Confucianism, the philosophy of the 5th-century B.C.
Chinese sage who taught that man can be perfected through practice.
"Confucius is not just some character out of the past—he is an every-
day reality to these people," said Willian Liu, a sociologist who
directs the Pacific Asian-American Mental Health Research Center at
the University of Illinois in Chicago.

Confucianism provides another important ingredient in the 20
Asians' success. "In the Confucian ethic," Liu continued, "there is a
centripetal family, an orientation that makes people work for the
honor of the family, not just for themselves." Liu came to the United
States from China in 1948. "You can never repay your parents, and
there is a strong sense of guilt," he said. "It is a strong force, like the
Protestant Ethic in the West."

Liu has found this in his own family. When his son and two 21
daughters were young, he told them to become doctors or lawyers—
jobs with the best guaranteed income, he felt. Sure enough, his
daughters have gone into law, and his son is a medical student at
UCLA, though he really wanted to be an investment banker. Liu
asked his son why he picked medicine. The reply: "Ever since I was

a little kid, I always heard you tell your friends their kids were a success if they got into med school. So I felt guilty. I didn't have a choice."

Underlying this bond between Asian parents and their children 22 is yet another factor I noticed during 15 years of living in China, Japan, Taiwan and Vietnam. It is simply that Asian parents establish a closer physical tie to their infants than do most parents in the United States. When I let my baby son and daughter crawl on the floor, for example, my Chinese friends were horrified and rushed to pick them up. We think this constant attention is overindulgence and old-fashioned, but for Asians, who still live through the lives of their children, it is highly effective.

Yuen Huo, 22, a senior at Berkeley, recalled growing up in an 23 apartment above the Chinese restaurant her immigrant parents owned and operated in Millbrae, Calif. "They used to tell us how they came from Taiwan to the United States for us, how they sacrificed for us, so I had a strong sense of indebtedness," Huo said. When she did not get all A's her first semester at Berkeley, she recalled, "I felt guilty and worked harder."

Here too is a vital clue about the Asians' success: Asian parents 24 expect a high level of academic performance. In the Stanford study comparing white and Asian students in San Francisco high schools, 82 percent of the Asian parents said they would accept only an A or a B from their children, while just 59 percent of white parents set such a standard. By comparison, only 17 percent of Asian parents were willing to accept a C, against 40 percent of white parents. On the average, parents of black and Hispanic students also had lower expectations for their children's grades than Asian parents.

Can we learn anything from the Asians? "I'm not naïve enough 25 to think everything in Asia can be transplanted," said Harold Stevenson, the University of Michigan psychologist. But he offered three recommendations.

"To start with," he said, "we need to set higher standards for our 26 kids. We wouldn't expect them to become professional athletes without practicing hard."

Second, American parents need to become more committed to 27 their children's education, he declared. "Being understanding when a child doesn't do well isn't enough." Stevenson found that Asian parents spend many more hours really helping their children with homework or writing to their teachers. At Berkeley, the mothers of some Korean-American students move into their sons' apartments for months before graduate school entrance tests to help by cooking and cleaning for them, giving the students more time to study.

And, third, schools could be reorganized to become more effective—without added costs, said Stevenson. One of his most surprising findings is that Asian students, contrary to popular myth, are not just rote learners subjected to intense pressure. Instead, nearly 90 percent of Chinese youngsters said they actually enjoy school, and 60 percent can't wait for school vacations to end. These are vastly higher figures for such attitudes than are found in the United States. One reason may be that students in China and Japan typically have a recess after each class; helping them to relax and to increase their attention spans. Moreover, where American teachers spend almost their entire day in front of classes, their Chinese and Japanese counterparts may teach as little as three hours a day, giving them more time to relax and prepare imaginative lessons. 28

Another study, prepared for the U.S. Department of Education, compared the math and science achievements of 24,000 13-year-olds in the United States and five other countries (four provinces of Canada, plus South Korea, Ireland, Great Britain and Spain). One of the findings was that the more time students spent watching television, the poorer their performance. The American students watched the most television. They also got the worst scores in math. Only the Irish students and some of the Canadians scored lower in science. 29

"I don't think Asians are any smarter," said Don Lee, the Korean-American at Berkeley. "There are brilliant Americans in my chemistry class. But the Asian students work harder. I see a lot of wasted potential among the Americans." 30

KID KUSTOMERS

Eric Schlosser

Twenty-five years ago, only a handful of American companies 1
directed their marketing at children—Disney, McDonald's, candy
makers, toy makers, manufacturers of breakfast cereal. Today children are being targeted by phone companies, oil companies, and
automobile companies as well as clothing stores and restaurant
chains. The explosion in children's advertising occurred during the
1980s. Many working parents, feeling guilty about spending less
time with their kids, started spending more money on them. One
marketing expert has called the 1980s "the decade of the child consumer." After largely ignoring children for years, Madison Avenue
began to scrutinize and pursue them. Major ad agencies now have
children's divisions, and a variety of marketing firms focus solely on
kids. These groups tend to have sweet-sounding names: Small Talk,
Kid Connection, Kid2Kid, the Gepetto Group, Just Kids, Inc. At least
three industry publications—*Youth Market Alert, Selling to Kids, and
Marketing to Kids Report*—cover the latest ad campaigns and market
research. The growth in children's advertising has been driven by
efforts to increase not just current, but also future, consumption.
Hoping that nostalgic childhood memories of a brand will lead to a
lifetime of purchases, companies now plan "cradle-to-grave" advertising strategies. They have come to believe what Ray Kroc and Walt
Disney realized long ago—a person's "brand loyalty" may begin as
early as the age of two. Indeed, market research has found that children often recognize a brand logo before they can recognize their
own name.

The discontinued Joe Camel ad campaign, which used a hip car- 2
toon character to sell cigarettes, showed how easily children can be
influenced by the right corporate mascot. A 1991 study published in
the *Journal of the American Medical Association* found that nearly all of
America's six-year-olds could identify Joe Camel, who was just as
familiar to them as Mickey Mouse. Another study found that one-
third of the cigarettes illegally sold to minors were Camels. More
recently, a marketing firm conducted a survey in shopping malls
across the country, asking children to describe their favorite TV ads.
According to the CME KidCom Ad Traction Study II, released at the
1999 Kids' Marketing Conference in San Antonio, Texas, the Taco Bell
commercials featuring a talking chihuahua were the most popular

fast food ads. The kids in the survey also like Pepsi and Nike commercials, but their favorite television ad was for Budweiser.

The bulk of the advertising directed at children today has an 3
immediate goal. "It's not just getting kids to whine," one marketer explained in *Selling to Kids*, "it's giving them a specific reason to ask for the product." Years ago sociologist Vance Packard described children as "surrogate salesmen" who had to persuade other people, usually their parents, to buy what they wanted. Marketers now use different terms to explain the intended response to their ads—such as "leverage," "the nudge factor," "pester power." The aim of most children's advertising is straightforward: Get kids to nag their parents and nag them well.

James U. McNeal, a professor of marketing at Texas A&M 4
University, is considered America's leading authority on marketing to children. In his book *Kids As Customers* (1992), McNeal provides marketers with a thorough analysis of "children's requesting styles and appeals." He classifies juvenile nagging tactics into seven major categories. A *pleading* nag is one accompanied by repetitions of words like "please" or "mom, mom, mom." A persistent nag involves constant requests for the coveted product and may include the phrase "I'm gonna ask just one more time." *Forceful* nags are extremely pushy and may include subtle threats, like "Well, then, I'll go and ask Dad." *Demonstrative* nags are the most high-risk, often characterized by full-blown tantrums in public places, breath-holding, tears, a refusal to leave the store. *Sugar-coated* nags promise affection in return for a purchase and may rely on seemingly heartfelt declarations like "You're the best dad in the world." *Threatening* nags are youthful forms of blackmail, vows of eternal hatred and of running away if something isn't bought. *Pity* nags claim the child will be heartbroken, teased, or socially stunted if the parent refuses to buy a certain item. "All of these appeals and styles may be used in combination," McNeal's research has discovered, "but kids tend to stick to one or two of each that proved most effective . . . for their own parents."

McNeal never advocates turning children into screaming, 5
breath-holding monsters. He has been studying "Kid Kustomers" for more than thirty years and believes in a more traditional marketing approach. "The key is getting children to see a firm . . . in much the same way as [they see] mom or dad, grandma or grandpa," McNeal argues. "Likewise, if a company can ally itself with universal values such as patriotism, national defense, and good health, it is likely to nurture belief in it among children."

Before trying to affect children's behavior, advertisers have to 6
learn about their tastes. Today's market researchers not only conduct
surveys of children in shopping malls, they also organize focus
groups for kids as young as two or three. They analyze children's art-
work, hire children to run focus groups, stage slumber parties and
then question children into the night. They send cultural anthropol-
ogists into homes, stores, fast food restaurants, and other places
where kids like to gather, quietly and surreptitiously observing the
behavior of prospective customers. They study the academic literature on child development, seeking insights from the work of theo-
rists such as Erik Erikson and Jean Piaget. They study the fantasy
lives of young children, they apply the findings in advertisements
and product designs.

Dan S. Acuff—the president of Youth Market System Consulting 7
and the author of *What Kids Buy and Why* (1997)—stresses the importance of dream research. Studies suggest that until the age of six,
roughly 80 percent of children's dreams are about animals. Rounded,
soft creatures like Barney, Disney's animated characters, and the
Teletubbies therefore have an obvious appeal to young children. The
Character Lab, a division of Youth Market System Consulting, uses a
proprietary technique called Character Appeal Quadrant analysis to
help companies develop new mascots. The technique purports to create imaginary characters who perfectly fit the targeted age group's
level of cognitive and neurological development.

Children's clubs have for years been considered an effective 8
means of targeting ads and collecting demographic information; the
clubs appeal to a child's fundamental need for status and belonging.
Disney's Mickey Mouse Club, formed in 1930, was one of the trail-
blazers. During the 1980s and 1990s, children's clubs proliferated, as
corporations used them to solicit the names, addresses, zip codes,
and personal comments of young customers. "Marketing messages
sent through a club not only can be personalized," James McNeal
advises, "they can be tailored for a certain age or geographical
group." A well-designed and well-run children's club can be
extremely good for business. According to one Burger King executive, the creation of a Burger King Kids Club in 1991 increased the
sales of children's meals as much as 300 percent.

The Internet has become another powerful tool for assembling 9
data about children. In 1998 a federal investigation of Web sites
aimed at children found that 89 percent requested personal information from kids; only 1 percent required that children obtain parental
approval before supplying the information. A character on the

McDonald's Web site told children that Ronald McDonald was "the ultimate authority in everything." The site encouraged kids to send Ronald an e-mail revealing their favorite menu item at McDonald's, their favorite book, their favorite sports team—and their name. Fast food Web sites no longer ask children to provide personal information without first gaining parental approval; to do so is now a violation of federal law, thanks to the Children's Online Privacy Protection Act, which took effect in April of 2000.

Despite the growing importance of the Internet, television 10 remains the primary medium for children's advertising. The effects of these TV ads have long been a subject of controversy. In 1978, the Federal Trade Commission (FTC) tried to ban all television ads directed at children seven years old or younger. Many studies had found that young children often could not tell the difference between television programming and television advertising. They also could not comprehend the real purpose of commercials and trusted that advertising claims were true. Michael Pertschuk, the head of the FTC, argued that children need to be shielded from advertising that preys upon their immaturity. "They cannot protect themselves," he said, "against adults who exploit their present-mindedness."

The FTC's proposed ban was supported by the American 11 Academy of Pediatrics, the National Congress of Parents and Teachers, the Consumers Union, and the Child Welfare League, among others. But it was attacked by the National Association of Broadcasters, the Toy Manufacturers of America, and the Association of National Advertisers. The industry groups lobbied Congress to prevent any restrictions on children's ads and sued in federal court to block Pertschuk from participating in future FTC meetings on the subject. In April of 1981, three months after the inauguration of President Ronald Reagan, an FTC staff report argued that a ban on ads aimed at children would be impractical, effectively killing the proposal. "We are delighted by the FTC's reasonable recommendation," said the head of the National Association of Broadcasters.

The Saturday-morning children's ads that caused angry debates 12 twenty years ago now seem almost quaint. Far from being banned, TV advertising aimed at kids is now broadcast twenty-four hours a day, closed-captioned and in stereo. Nickelodeon, the Disney Channel, the Cartoon Network, and the other children's cable networks are now responsible for about 80 percent of all television viewing by kids. None of these networks existed before 1979. The typical American child now spends about twenty-one hours a week watching television—roughly one and a half months of TV every year. That does not include the time children spend in front of a screen watching videos, playing video games, or using the computer. Outside of school, the typical American child spends more time watching television than doing any other activity except sleeping. During the course of a year, he or she watches more than thirty thousand TV commercials. Even the nation's youngest children are watching a great deal of television. About one-quarter of American children between the ages of two and five have a TV in their room.

4

EXPLAINING

THE ORIGINS OF ANOREXIA NERVOSA

Joan Jacobs Brumberg

Contrary to the popular assumption that anorexia nervosa is a 1
peculiarly modern disorder, the malady first emerged in the
Victorian era—long before the pervasive cultural imperative for a
thin female body. The first clinical descriptions of the disorder
appeared in England and France almost simultaneously in 1873.
They were written by two well-known physicians: Sir William
Withey Gull and Charles Lasègue. Lasègue, more than any other
nineteenth-century doctor, captured the rhythm of repeated offerings
and refusals that signaled the breakdown of reciprocity between parents and their anorexic daughter. By returning to its origins, we can
see anorexia nervosa for what it is: a dysfunction in the bourgeois
family system.

Family meals assumed enormous importance in the bourgeois 2
milieu, in the United States as well as in England and France.
Middle-class parents prided themselves on providing ample food for
their children. The abundance of food and the care in its preparation
became expressions of social status. The ambience of the meal sym-
bolized the values of the family. A popular domestic manual advised,
"Simple, healthy food, exquisitely prepared, and served upon shin-
ing dishes and brilliant silverware . . . a gentle blessing, and cheerful
conversation, embrace the sweetest communions and the happiest
moments of life." Among the middle class it seems that eating correctly was emerging as a new morality, one that set its members apart
from the working class.

At the same time, food was used to express love in the nineteenth- 3
century bourgeois household. Offering attractive and abundant meals

51

was the particular responsibility and pleasure of middle-class wives and mothers. In America the feeding of middle-class children, from infancy on, had become a maternal concern no longer deemed appropriate to delegate to wet nurses, domestics, or governesses. Family meals were expected to be a time of instructive and engaging conversation. Participation was expected on both a verbal and gustatory level. In this context, refusing to eat was an unabashedly antisocial act. Anorexic behavior was antithetical to the ideal of bourgeois eating. One advice book, *Common Sense for Maid, Wife, and Mother*, stated: "Heated discussion and quarrels, fretfulness and sullen taciturnity while eating, are as unwholesome as they are unchristian."

Why would a daughter affront her parents by refusing to eat? Lasègue's 1873 description of anorexia nervosa, along with other nineteenth-century medical reports, suggests that pressure to marry may have precipitated the illness. 4

Ambitious parents surely understood that by marrying well, at an appropriate moment, a daughter, even though she did not carry the family name, could help advance a family's social status—particularly in a burgeoning middle-class society. As a result, the issue of marriage loomed large in the life of a dutiful middle-class daughter. Although marriage did not generally occur until the girl's early twenties, it was an event for which she was continually prepared, and a desirable outcome for all depended on the ability of the parents and the child to work together—that is, to state clearly what each wanted or to read each other's heart and mind. In the context of marital expectations, a daughter's refusal to eat was a provocative rejection of both the family's social aspirations and their goodwill toward her. All of the parents' plans for her future (and their own) could be stymied by her peculiar and unpleasant alimentary nihilism. 5

Beyond the specific anxieties generated by marital pressure, the Victorian family milieu in America and in Western Europe harbored a mélange of other tensions and problems that provided the emotional preconditions for the emergence of anorexia nervosa. As love replaced authority as the cement of family relations, it began to generate its own set of emotional disorders. 6

Possessiveness, for example, became an acute problem in Victorian family life. Where love between parents and children was the prevailing ethic, there was always the risk of excess. When love became suffocating or manipulative, individuation and separation from the family could become extremely painful, if not impossible. In the context of increased intimacy, adolescent privacy was especially problematic: For parents and their sexually maturing daughters, 7 what constituted an appropriate degree of privacy? Middle-class girls, for example, almost always had their own rooms or shared them with sisters, but they had greater difficulty establishing autonomous psychic space. The well-known penchant of adolescent girls for novel-reading was an expression of their need for imaginative freedom. Some parents, recognizing that their daughters needed channels for expressing emotions, encouraged diary-keeping. But some of the same parents who gave lovely marbled journals as gifts also monitored their content. Since emotional freedom was not an acknowledged prerogative of the Victorian adolescent girl, it seems likely that she would have expressed unhappiness in non-verbal forms of behavior. One such behavior was refusal of food.

When an adolescent daughter became sullen and chronically 8 refused to eat, her parents felt threatened and confused. The daughter was perceived as willfully manipulating her appetite the way a younger child might. Because parents did not want to encourage this behavior, they often refused at first to indulge the favorite tastes or caprices of their daughter. As emaciation became visible and the girl looked ill, many violated the contemporary canon of prudent child-rearing and put aside their moral objections to pampering the appetite. Eventually they would beg their daughter to eat whatever she liked—and eat she must, "as a sovereign proof of affection" for them. From the parents' perspective, a return to eating was a confirmation of filial love.

The significance of food refusal as an emotional tactic within the 9 family depended on food's being plentiful, pleasing, and connected to love. Where food was eaten simply to assuage hunger, where it had only minimal aesthetic and symbolic messages, or where the girl had to provide her own nourishment, refusal of food was not particularly noteworthy or defiant. In contrast, the anorexic girl was surrounded by a provident, if not indulgent, family that was bound to be distressed by her rejection of its largess.

Anorexia nervosa was an intense form of discourse that honored 10 the emotional guidelines that governed the middle-class Victorian family. Refusing to eat was not as confrontational as yelling, having a tantrum, or throwing things; refusing to eat expressed emotional hostility without being flamboyant. And refusing to eat had the advantage of being ambiguous. If a girl repeatedly claimed lack of appetite she might indeed be ill and therefore entitled to special treatment and favors.

In her own way, the anorexic was respectful of what historian 11 Peter Gay called "the great bourgeois compromise between the need for reserve and the capacity for emotion." The rejection of food, while an emotionally charged behavior, was also discreet, quiet, and lady-like. The unhappy adolescent who was in all other ways a dutiful daughter chose food refusal from within the symptom repertoire available to her. Precisely because she was not a lunatic, she selected a behavior that she knew would have some efficacy within her own family.

LIES, LIES, LIES

Paul Gray

The injunction against bearing false witness, branded in stone 1 and brought down by Moses from the mountaintop, has always provoked ambivalent, conflicting emotions. On the one hand, nearly everyone condemns lying. On the other, nearly everyone does it every day. How many of the Ten Commandments can be broken so easily and with so little risk of detection over the telephone?

Hence the never-ending paradox: some bedrock of honesty is 2 fundamental to society; people cannot live together if no one is able to believe what anyone else is saying. But there also seems to be an honesty threshold, a point beyond which a virtue turns mean and nasty. Constantly hearing the truth, the cold, hard, brutal unsparing truth, from spouses, relatives, friends and colleagues is not a pleasant prospect. "Humankind," as T. S. Eliot wrote, "cannot bear very much reality." Truth telling makes it possible for people to coexist; a little lying makes such society tolerable.

At what point does "a little" become "too much"? The nervous 3 boy who cried "Wolf!" in the admonitory tale told one lie too many and was eaten alive. The irony of this dénouement, of course, is that when the boy met his fate, he was, at last, hollering the truth.

This story demonstrates the creation of what is sometimes, and 4 euphemistically, called "a climate of mistrust." (Translation: Everybody's lying.) It also reveals how difficult it is for those in the vicinity of a lie to distinguish it from the truth.

That task would be easy if humans resembled Pinocchio (as 5 Clinton claims Bush does), with their noses growing longer each time they told a lie. People, unfortunately, can fib without suffering physiognomic changes. It would be helpful, then, if there were some hidden manifestation of lying, invisible to most people but clear to psychics or visionaries. The closest that real life has managed to come to this fictional power is the polygraph machine, which has a few serious drawbacks. It can be stumped by accomplished actors or those delusional enough to believe their own statements, and even experts disagree on the machine's level of reliability. And lie detectors, of course, are impractical to haul out on nearly all the occasions—including first dates, tax audits, political rallies—when they might prove handy.

Public perceptions to the contrary, it is impossible to prove that more people are lying than did in the past. There is no central clearinghouse of lies, no impartial scorekeeper deciding on the truth or falsity of public statements. Further complicating matters, successful lies, by definition, go undetected. If this truly is a time of unprecedented public lying, then it is also a time of remarkably inept liars, or of liars who don't seem to care if they are caught. 6

Certainty about lying is suspect because the practice is extraordinarily complex. Discussions of the subject usually begin with the assumption that everyone present agrees on what a lie actually is. A lie happens, a rough definition might assert, when someone does not tell the truth. Unfortunately, the relationship between lying and the truth is nowhere near this simple. A false statement need not be a lie. "The earth is flat," coming from a member of the Flat Earth Society, is not a lie but a statement of belief. Furthermore, a true statement can be a lie. Imagine a dishonest agent telling a client, "The check is in the mail," and then discovering to his horror that his new secretary has actually . . . mailed the check. Even though his client got paid, the agent intended to lie. 7

So objective truth is an unreliable standard against which lies can be measured. Most lies, of course, involve a distortion of the truth, but so do many innocent remarks. And the notorious difficulty of getting at the truth works to the liar's advantage; since there are so many different versions of reality floating around, another one, invented, won't do any harm—and may even be more entertaining to boot. 8

Fortunately, there is a way out of this logical blind alley. All lies, regardless of their relationship to the truth, have one thing in common. "We must single out," writes Sissela Bok in *Lying*, "from the countless ways in which we blunder misinformed through life, that which is done with the *intention to mislead.*" Lies may confuse everyone who hears them, as they are meant to, but liars know exactly what they are doing while they are doing it. In *Telling Lies*, Paul Ekman, a professor of psychology at the University of California medical school in San Francisco, provides a slightly more elaborate definition: "One person intends to mislead another, doing so deliberately, without prior notification of this purpose, and without having been explicitly asked to do so by the target. There are two primary ways to lie: to *conceal* and to *falsify.*" 9

Ekman's formula is helpful, within limits. It defines the contexts in which lies are or are not improper. It absolves actors and fiction writers, for example, whose professions involve fabrications but 10 whose audiences are presumably aware of this condition before they go to the theater or open a book. But problems arise with Ekman's notion that lying can be an act of concealment alone. Is not publicizing the possible dangers, say, of silicone breast implants in and of itself a lie? Or does this concealment merely set the stage for the true, dangerous deception, the impression created by the manufacturer in the enforced absence of information that such implants are safe? When a wife asks her husband how his day went, is he obliged to answer, "Great—I spent the lunch hour in a motel room with my mistress"? If he does not disclose this detail, is he guilty of lying, or is he—the cheat—simply sparing his wife's feelings or avoiding a potentially unpleasant scene?

Not everyone agrees on the answers to these and similar questions. Every lie—save those of self-deception—involves two or more people in an intricate arabesque of intentions and expectations. What does the person telling a lie hope to achieve? How do the recipients of the lie understand it? What, in short, do all the parties involved think is happening? 11

St. Augustine identified eight kinds of lies, not all of them equally serious but all sins nonetheless. The number Mark Twain came up with, not too seriously, was 869. In practice, there are probably as many lies as there are liars, but lying can be roughly classified according to motive and context. No hard boundaries exist between these categories, since some lies are told for more than one purpose. But most of them fall within a spectrum of three broad categories. 12

1. Lies to protect others, or "I love your dress." Most "little white lies" belong here, well-intentioned deceptions designed to grease the gears of society. In this context, people want to be fooled. No one expects, and few would welcome, searing honesty at a dinner party. And the couple who leave early, saying the babysitter has a curfew, would not be thanked by the hostess if the truth were told: "Frankly, we're both bored to tears." 13

On rare occasions, lying to protect others can literally be a matter of life or death. Anne Frank survived as long as she did because those sheltering her and her family lied to the Nazis. The French Resistance during World War II could not have operated without deception. Military and intelligence officials will as a matter of routine lie to protect secret plans or agents at risk. 14

Few would condemn such protective lies. But problems arise when the alleged noble purpose of a lie loses the clarity, say, of saving innocent lives and gets muddled by other considerations. National security has been a notorious refuge for scoundrels who 15 confuse their interests with their country's and therefore lie to cover up both. Convinced that winning the Vietnam War was essential to U.S. interests, President Lyndon Johnson was exasperated to learn that not all Americans agreed with him. These ignorant, shortsighted people therefore had to be protected from themselves, an end that justified almost any means. The long trail of lies and deceptions that followed is a lamentable matter of record.

2. **Lies in the interest of the liar, or "The dog ate my home-** 16 **work."** Here rest the domains, familiar to everyone, of being on the spot, of feeling guilty, of fearing reprimand, failure or disgrace, and on the other side of the ledger, of wishing to seem more impressive to others than the bald facts will allow. Complicity between liar and auditor rarely occurs in this category; the liar wants to get away with something. If a lie turneth away wrath, or wins a job or a date on Saturday night, why not tell it? Because to do so is immoral and wrong, runs the standard, timeworn answer. But this stricture has never cut as much ice with potential liars as moralists would wish. The vast majority of criminal defendants assert their innocence, no matter what the evidence against them. Watergate was a baroque pageant of major players and spear carriers trying to lie themselves out of jeopardy.

Greed ranks right up there with guilt as an inducement to lie. The 17 S & L debacle and the Wall Street insider trading scandals of the late 1980s involved exquisitely complex patterns of lies and deceptions. These fiascos harmed thousands of investors and left taxpayers with a staggering bill to pay, but that was not their intent. The purpose of the lies told in these massive scams was to enrich the perpetrators.

Lies in the interest of liars may also extend to those with whom 18 the liars feel closely bound—the individual to his tribe, sect, community or nation, the employee to his employers, the professional to his peers, the advertiser or lawyer to his client. If collective success or profit is a paramount goal, a lie told to achieve it may seem a tempting alternative.

3. **Lies to cause harm, or "Trust me on this one."** The role model 19 here is Shakespeare's Iago, insidiously, malevolently and falsely poisoning Othello's mind against his faithful wife Desdemona. These are the lies people fear and resent the most, statements that will not only deceive them but also trick them into foolish or ruinous courses of behavior. Curiously, though, lying to hurt people just for the hell or the fun of it—the Iago syndrome—is probably quite rare. Though Samuel Taylor Coleridge wrote influentially about Iago's "motiveless malignity," the play itself does not really support this judgment. Iago

has a motive, all right: he believes Othello has unfairly passed him over for a promotion, and he wants revenge. Some perceived advantage prompts most lies. If there is no benefit in telling a lie, most people won't bother to make one up.

Lies flourish in social uncertainty, when people no longer understand, or agree on, the rules governing their behavior toward one another. During such periods, skepticism also increases; there will be a perception that more people are lying, whether or not they actually are. That seems to be what is happening now.   20

The weakening of the major parties and the rise of television have made politics an infinitely more difficult—and morally tenuous—endeavor. It is no longer sufficient for candidates to say they are Democrats or Republicans, explain their views on the issues and let the voters decide. Campaigns now consist of offending as few people as possible, so the possibilities for mischief and misunderstandings are endless.   21

Politicians know they are widely perceived as liars. They also remember what happened to presidential nominee Walter Mondale after he told the 1984 Democratic National Convention that he would, if elected, raise taxes. Voters say they want the truth, and then they get angry when they hear it.   22

Furthermore, the prolonged recession has created endemic anxieties. If survival seems to hang on getting an edge, cutting a corner, telling a lie, then many otherwise moral people will choose to survive. The economy will, of course, improve; but the hangover from the recession may stick around: the impression that doing business, earning a living, is a con game, with rewards going to the clever and the unscrupulous.   33

Finally, a phenomenon has become so pervasive that it almost goes unnoticed. Everyone seems to have got incredibly nosy. The press is part of this problem, particularly the aggressive new tabloid and infotainment TV shows. But reporters would not yell intrusive questions if they knew their readers or viewers did not care about the answers.   24

After Vietnam, Watergate, Iran-*contra*, and the Gary Hart indiscretion, it is hard to make a case against the public's right to know. But not impossible. Candor is necessary when it really matters, and little more than a nuisance when it doesn't. At the moment, people are unsure which is which. A lie may be a defensive response to an unwarranted invasion of privacy. The oddity that Oprah and Phil and Geraldo can attract guests willing to confess anything on TV does not oblige everyone else to bare all when asked.   25

St. Augustine defined all lies as sins because they misused God's 26
gift of speech. In a better world than this one, people would agree
and act accordingly. In fact, in a better world lies would not be necessary at all, since the truth would be self-evident and foolish to deny
or attempt to refute. The world we have discourages such certainties.
Lies will continue to be told, as will the difficulty of recognizing them
as such. But some modicum of trust will probably also survive, as it
has through notable periods of lying in the past. When the perception
of lying grows too acute, some shift, some click in the social consciousness, takes place: Danger ahead. The bad, suspicious mood of
this political year is a sign of health, a recognition that the private
advantages of lying are being eclipsed by the communal necessity to
tell—or to try to tell—the truth.

THE RHETORIC OF ADVERTISING

Stuart Hirschberg

Whether ads are presented as sources of information enabling 1
the consumer to make educated choices between products or aim at
offering memorable images or witty, thoughtful, or poetic copy, the
underlying intent of all advertising is to persuade specific audiences.
Seen in this way, ads appear as mini-arguments whose strategies and
techniques of persuasion can be analyzed just like a written argument. We can discover which elements are designed to appeal to the
audience's emotions (*pathos* according to Aristotle), which elements
make their appeal in terms of reasons, evidence, or logic (*logos*), and
how the advertiser goes about winning credibility for itself or in
terms of the spokesperson employed to speak on behalf of the product (the *ethos* dimension). Like arguments, ads can be effective if they
appeal to the needs, values, and beliefs of the audience. Although the
verbal and visual elements within an ad are designed to work
together, we can study these elements separately. We can look at how
the composition of the elements within an ad is intended to function.
We can look at the role of language and how it is used to persuade.
We can study how objects and settings are used to promote the audience's identification with the products being sold. We can judge ads
according to the skill with which they deploy all of these resources
while at the same time being critically aware of their intended effects
on us.

The Techniques of Advertising

The claim the ad makes is designed to establish the superiority of 2
the product in the minds of the audience and to create a distinctive
image for the product, whether it is a brand of cigarettes, a financial
service, or a type of gasoline. The single most important technique
for creating this image depends on transferring ideas, attributes, or
feelings from outside the product onto the product itself. In this way
the product comes to represent an obtainable object or service that
embodies, represents, or symbolizes a whole range of meanings. This
transfer can be achieved in many ways. For example, when Nicole
Kidman or Jennifer Lopez lends her glamour and beauty to the mer-
chandising of a perfume, the consumer is meant to conclude that the

perfume must be superior to other perfumes in the way that the actress embodies beauty, glamour, and sex appeal. The attempt to transfer significance can operate in two ways. It can encourage the audience to discover meanings and to correlate feelings and attributes that the advertiser wishes the product to represent in ways that allow these needs and desires to become attached to specific products. It can also prevent the correlation of thoughts or feelings that might discourage the audience from purchasing a particular product. For example, the first most instinctive response to the thought of smoking a cigarette might be linked with the idea of inhaling hot and dry smoke from what are essentially burning tobacco leaves. Thus, any associations the audience might have with burning leaves, coughing, and dry hot smoke must be short-circuited by supplying them with a whole set of other associations to receive and occupy the perceptual "slot" that might have been triggered by their first reactions. Cigarette advertisers do this in a variety of ways:

> By showing active people in outdoorsy settings, they put the thought of emphysema, shortness of breath, or lung disease very far away indeed.
>
> By showing cigarette packs set against the background of grass glistening with morning dew or bubbling streams or cascading waterfalls, they subtly guide the audience's response away from what is dry, hot, congested, or burning toward what is open, airy, moist, cool, and clean.
>
> In some brands, menthol flavoring and green and blue colors are intended to promote these associations.

Thus, ads act as do all other kinds of persuasion to intensify correlations that work to the advertiser's advantage and to suppress associations that would lessen the product's appeal. 3

The kinds of associations audiences are encouraged to perceive 4 reflect a broad range of positive emotional appeals that encourage the audience to find self-esteem through the purchase of a product that by itself offers a way to meet personal and social needs. The particular approach taken in the composition of the ad, the way it is laid out, and the connotations of the advertising copy vary according to the emotional appeal of the ad.

The most common manipulative techniques are designed to 5 make consumers want to consume to satisfy deep-seated human drives. Of course, no one consciously believes that purchasing a particular kind of toothpaste, perfume, lipstick, or automobile will meet real psychological and social needs, but that is exactly how products are sold—through the promise of delivering unattainable satisfactions through tangible purchasable objects or services. In purchasing a certain product, we are offered the chance to create ourselves, our personality, and our relationships through consumption.

Emotional Appeals Used in Advertising

The emotional appeals in ads function exactly the way assumptions about value do in written arguments. They supply the unstated major premise that supplies a rationale to persuade an audience that a particular product will meet one or another of several different kinds of needs. Some ads present the purchase of a product as a means by which consumers can find social acceptance. 6

These ads address the consumer as "you" ("Wouldn't 'you' really rather have a Buick?"). The "you" here is plural but is perceived as being individual and personal by someone who has already formed the connection with the product. Ironically, the price of remaining in good standing with this "group" of fellow consumers requires the consumer to purchase an expensive automobile. In this sense, ads give consumers a chance to belong to social groups that have only one thing in common—the purchase of a particular product. 7

One variation on the emotional need to belong to a designated social group is the appeal to status or "snob appeal." Snob appeal is not new. In 1710, the *Spectator*, a popular newspaper of the time, carried an ad that read: 8

> An incomparable Powder for Cleaning Teeth, which has given great satisfaction to most of the Nobility Gentry in England.

Ads for scotch, expensive cars, boats, jewelry, and watches frequently place their products in upper-class settings or depict them in connection with the fine arts (sculpture, ballet, etc.). The *value warrant* in these ads encourages the consumer to imagine that the purchase of the item will confer qualities associated with the background or activities of this upper-class world onto the consumer. 9

In other ads the need to belong takes a more subtle form of offering the product as a way to become part of a time in the past the audience might look back to with nostalgia. Grandmotherly figures wearing aprons and holding products that are advertised as being "like Grandma used to make" offer the consumer an imaginary past, a family tradition, or a simpler time looked back to with warmth and sentimentality. For many years, Smucker's preserves featured ads in 10 which the product was an integral part of a scene emanating security and warmth, which the ad invited us to remember as if it were our own past. Ads of this kind are often photographed through filters that present misty sepia-tone images that carefully recreate old-fashioned kitchens with the accompanying appliances, dishes, clothes, and hairstyles. The ads thus supply us with false memories and invite us to insert ourselves into this imaginary past and to remember it as if it were our own. At the furthest extreme, ads employing the appeal to see ourselves as part of a group may try to evoke patriotic feelings so that the prospective consumer will derive the satisfactions of good citizenship and sense of participation in being part of the collective psyche of an entire nation. The point is that people really do have profound needs that advertisers can exploit, but it would be a rare product indeed that could really fulfill such profound needs.

Advertisers use highly sophisticated market research techniques 11 to enable them to define and characterize precisely those people who are most likely to be receptive to ads of particular kinds. The science of demographics is aided and abetted by psychological research that enables advertisers to "target" a precisely designated segment of the general public. For example, manufacturers of various kinds of liquor can rely on studies that inform them that vodka drinkers are most likely to read *Psychology Today* and scotch drinkers the *New Yorker*, while readers of *Time* prefer rum and the audience for *Playboy* has a large number of readers who prefer gin. Once a market segment with defined psychological characteristics has been identified, an individual ad can be crafted for that particular segment and placed in the appropriate publication.

Ads, of course, can elicit responses by attempting to manipulate 12 consumers through negative as well as positive emotional appeals. Helen Woodward, the head copywriter for an ad agency, once offered the following advice for ad writers trying to formulate a new ad for baby food: "Give 'em the figures about the baby death rate—but don't say it flatly . . . if we only had the nerve to put a hearse in the ad, you couldn't keep the women away from the food" (Stuart Ewen, *Captains of Consciousness: Advertising and the Social Roots of Consumer Culture* [1976]). Ads of this kind must first arouse the consumer's anxieties and then offer the product as the solution to the problem that more often than not the ad has created.

For example, an advertisement for Polaroid evokes the fear of not 13 having taken pictures of moments that cannot be re-created and then offers the product as a form of insurance that will prevent this calamity from occurring. Nikon does the same in claiming that "a moment is called a moment because it doesn't last forever. Think of sunsets. A child's surprise. A Labrador's licky kiss. This is precisely why the Nikon N50 has the simple 'Simple' switch on top of the camera."

Ads for products that promise to guarantee their purchasers sex 14 appeal, youth, health, social acceptance, self-esteem, creativity, enlightenment, a happy family life, loving relationships, escape from boredom, vitality, and many other things frequently employ scare tactics to frighten or worry the consumer into purchasing the product to ease his or her fears. These ads must first make the consumer dissatisfied with the self that exists. In this way, they function exactly as do *policy arguments* that recommend solutions to problems with measurably harmful consequences. The difference is that these kinds of ads actually are designed to arouse and then exploit the anxieties related to these problems.

Large industrial conglomerates, whether in oil, chemicals, phar- 15 maceuticals, or agribusiness, frequently use advertising to accomplish different kinds of objectives than simply persuading the consumer to buy a particular product. These companies often seek to persuade the general public that they are not polluting the environment, poisoning the water, or causing environmental havoc in the process of manufacturing their products. The emotional appeal they use is to portray themselves as concerned "corporate citizens," vitally interested in the public good as a whole, and especially in those communities where they conduct their operations. In some cases, the ads present products as if they were directly produced from nature without being subjected to intermediary processing, preservatives, and contaminants, thereby lessening concern that they produce harmful byproducts. For example, Mazola might depict a spigot producing corn oil directly inserted into an ear of corn. A Jeep might appear to have materialized out of thin air on a seemingly inaccessible mountain peak. Companies sensitive to accusations that they are polluting the air and water can mount an advertising campaign designed to prove that they are not simply exploiting the local resources (whether timber, oil, fish, coal) for profits but are genuinely interested in putting something back into the community. The folksy good-neighbor tone of these ads is designed to create a benign image of the company.

The Language of Advertising

We can see how the creation of a sense of the company's credi- 16 bility as a concerned citizen corresponds to what Aristotle called the *ethos* dimension. For example, Chevron expresses concern that the light from their oil drilling operations be shielded so that spawning sea turtles won't be unintentionally misdirected and lose their way!

The appeals to logic, statements of reasons, and presentations of 17 evidence in ads correspond to the *logos* dimension of argument. The wording of the claims is particularly important, since it determines whether companies are legally responsible for any claims they make.

Claims in advertising need to be evaluated to discover whether 18 something is asserted that needs to be proved or is implied without actually being stated.

Claims may refer to authoritative-sounding results obtained by 19 supposedly independent laboratories, teams of research scientists, or physicians without ever saying how these surveys were conducted, what statistical methods were used, and who interpreted the results. Ads of this kind may make an impressive-sounding quasi-scientific claim; Ivory Soap used to present itself as "99 and 44/100% pure" without answering "pure" what. Some ads use technical talk and scientific terms to give the impression of a scientific breakthrough. For example, STP claims that it added "an anti-wear agent and viscosity improvers" to your oil. The copy for L. L. Bean claims of one of its jackets that "even in brutal ice winds gusting to 80 knots this remarkable anorak kept team members who wore it warm and comfortable." It would be important to know that the team members referred to are members of the "L. L. Bean test team."

Other claims cannot be substantiated, for example, "we're the 20 Dexter Shoe Company. And for nearly four decades we put a lot of Dexter Maine into every pair of shoes we make."

In an ad for lipstick, Aveda makes the claim that "it's made 21 of rich, earthy lip colours formulated with pure plant pigment from the Uruku tree. Organically grown by indigenous people in the rain forest."

Claims may be deceptive in other ways. Of all the techniques 22 advertisers use to influence what people believe and how they spend their money, none is more basic than the use of so-called *weasel words*. This term was popularized by Theodore Roosevelt in a speech he gave in St. Louis, May 31, 1916, when he commented that notes from the Department of State were filled with weasel words that retract the meaning of the words they are next to just as a weasel sucks the meat out of the egg.

In modern advertising parlance, a weasel word has come to 23 mean any qualifier or comparative that is used to imply a positive

quality that cannot be stated as a fact, because it cannot be substantiated. For example, if an ad claims a toothpaste will "help" stop cavi-
ties it does not obligate the manufacturer to substantiate this claim.
So, too, if a product is advertised as "fighting" germs, the equivocal
claim hides the fact that the product may fight and lose.

An ad for STP claimed that "no matter what kind of car you 24
drive, STP gas treatment helps remove the water that leads to gas line
freeze. And unlike gas line anti-freeze, our unique gas treatment formula works to reduce intake valve deposits and prevent clogged
injectors." The key words are "helps" and "works," neither of which
obligates STP to be legally accountable to support the claim.

The words *virtually* (as in "virtually spotless") and *up to or for as* 25
long as (as in "stops coughs up to eight hours") also remove any legal
obligation on the part of the manufacturer to justify the claim.

Other favorite words in the copywriter's repertoire, such as *free* 26
and *new*, are useful in selling everything from cat food to political
candidates.

The Ethical Dimension of Persuasion

As we have seen in our examination of the methods advertisers 27
use to influence consumers, ethical questions are implicit in every act
of persuasion. For example, what are we to make of a persuader
whose objectives in seeking to influence an audience may be praise-
worthy but who consciously makes use of distorted facts or seeks to
manipulate an audience by playing on their known attitudes, values,
and beliefs? Is success in persuasion the only criterion or should we
hold would-be persuaders accountable to some ethical standards of
responsibility about the means they use to achieve specific ends?
Perhaps the most essential quality in determining whether any act of
persuasion is an ethical one depends on the writer maintaining an
open dialogue with different perspectives that might be advanced on
a particular issue. By contrast, any act of persuasion that intention-
ally seeks to avoid self-criticism or challenges from competing perspectives will come across as insincere, dogmatic, deceptive, and
defensive. The desire to shut down debate or control an audience's
capacity to respond to the argument might well be considered unethical. The consequence of this attitude may be observed in the arguer's
use of fraudulent evidence, illogical reasoning, emotionally laden
irrelevant appeals, simplistic representation of the issue, or the pre-

tense of expertise. Standards to apply when judging the ethical dimension in any act of persuasion require us to consider whether any element of coercion, deception, or manipulation is present. This becomes especially true when we look at the relationship between propaganda as a form of mass persuasion and the rhetorical means used to influence large groups of people.

5

EVALUATING

ALL'S NOT WELL IN LAND OF "THE LION KING"

Margaret Lazarus

It's official: Walt Disney's *The Lion King* is breaking box-office 1
records. Unfortunately, it's not breaking any stereotypes.

My sons, along with millions of other kids around the world, joy- 2
ously awaited *The Lion King*. I was intrigued because this time Disney
appeared to be skipping the old folk-tales with their traditional and
primal undercurrents.

I hoped Disney had grown weary of reinforcing women's subor- 3
dinate status by screening fables about a beauty who tames an angry
male beast or a mermaid who gives up her glorious voice and splits
her body to be with a prince.

So off we went to the movies, figuring we would enjoy an origi- 4
nal, well-animated story about animals on the African plain. Even
before the title sequence, however, I started to shudder.

Picture this (and I apologize for spilling the plot): The golden- 5
maned—that is, good—lion is presenting his first born male child to
his subjects. All the animals in the kingdom, known as Pride Lands,
are paying tribute to the infant son that will someday be their king.
These royal subjects are basically lion food—zebras, monkeys, birds,
etc.—and they all live together in supposed harmony in the "circle of
life."

Outside the kingdom, in a dark, gloomy, and impoverished ele- 6
phant graveyard, are the hyenas. They live dismally jammed
together among bones and litter. The hyenas are dark—mostly
black—and they are nasty, menacing the little lion prince when he
wanders into their territory.

One of their voices is done by Whoopie Goldberg, in a clearly 7
inner-city dialect. If this is not the ghetto, I don't know what is.

All is not perfect inside Pride Lands, however. The king's evil 8
brother Scar has no lionesses or cubs. Scar has a black mane, and
speaks in an effeminate, limp-pawed, British style done by Jeremy
Irons—seemingly a gay caricature.

Scar conspires with the hyenas to kill the king and send the 9
prince into exile. In exchange for their support, Scar allows the hyenas to live in Pride Lands. But property values soon crash: The hyenas overpopulate, kill all the game, and litter the once-green land
with bones.

Already Disney has gays and blacks ruining the "natural order," 10
and the stereotypes keep rolling. The lionesses never question
whether they should be serving Scar and the hyenas—they just
worry a lot. They are mistreated, but instead of fighting back these
powerful hunters passively await salvation. (Even my 7-year-old
wondered why the young, strong lioness didn't get rid of Scar.)

The circle of life is broken; disaster awaits everyone. But then the 11
first-born male returns to reclaim power. The royal heir kills the gay
usurper, and sends the hyenas back to the dark, gloomy, bone-filled
ghetto. Order is restored and the message is clear: Only those born to
privilege can bring about change.

This is not a story about animals—we know animals don't 12
behave like this. This is a metaphor for society that originated in the
minds of Disney's creators. These bigoted images and attitudes will
lodge deeply in children's consciousness.

I'm not sure I always understand the law of the Hollywood jun- 13
gle, but my boys definitely don't. Scared and frightened by *The Lion
King*, they were also riveted, and deeply affected. But entranced by
the "Disney magic," they and millions of other children were given
hidden messages that can only do them—and us—harm.

ANDY WARHOL: THE MOST CONTROVERSIAL ARTIST OF THE TWENTIETH CENTURY

Alan Pratt

When Andy Warhol hit his stride in the early sixties by appro- 1
priating images from advertising design and serializing them with a
hands-off austerity, he became a lightning rod for criticism.

Studying the public perception of the artist in 1966, critic Lucy 2
Lippard noticed that "Warhol's films and his art mean either nothing
or a great deal. The choice is the viewer's. . . ." In retrospect,
Lippard's early, tentative appraisal is revealing. While the images
Warhol stumbled across have a deep resonance with the public, the
problem of interpreting them is, depending one's point of view, simple or complex.

In the current polemic, Warhol's reputation still depends on the 3
reviewer's ideological or art-historical preoccupations. If, as has been
suggested, Warhol succeeded in redefining the art experience, then
the critical response required redefinition as well. In retrospect, it
appears that one problem that confronted critics and journalists was
that established critical approaches simply didn't lend themselves to
an art which they perceived as "artless, styleless, and anonymous."

While the debate still hasn't resolved itself, three interconnected 4
issues figure prominently in the disagreements about Warhol's reputation: his persona, his originality, and his antecedents.

Warhol's Persona

The problematic nature of Warhol's critical reputation is attribut- 5
able, in part, to the evasive, equivocal persona he cultivated—the calculated indifference, the monosyllabic rejoinder, the flat, vacuous
affect of the I-think-everybody-should-be-a-machine Warhol. And
while it's true that he suffered from a debilitating shyness, he never-
theless delighted in baffling his critics.

In reviewing Warhol's life it's often impossible to distinguish the 6
authentic Warhol from the act. As a result, a significant portion of the
critical response, if only anecdotally, is to Warhol's personality. And
with little that's reliable to go on, critics have wide latitude in extrap-
olating or inventing motives for him. Currently, psychological inter-
pretations of Warhol's work are the fashion.

71

Warhol's Originality

Like the problems of personality which have intrigued critics for 7 years, the issue of Warhol's artistic legitimacy has also been the basis of ongoing debate. The subjects of some of his most famous works—the soup cans, Coke bottles, dollar bills, flowers, and cows—were apparently recommendations.

That Warhol borrowed his images from others, from pho- 8 tographs, advertisements, and food labels and developed a technique by which they were serially mass-produced by anonymous Factory hands remains one of the most contentious issues in the criticism.

By erasing himself from his creations, minimizing the artist's 9 responsibility, the significance of talent, and the value of originality, Warhol challenged presumptions about what art is supposed to be and how one is to experience it. This abnegation of responsibility was deemed unethical, if not subversive, by the critical audience, further fueling the controversy about whether or not his work should even be regarded as art.

Warhol's Antecedents

From the beginning, critics have addressed the connections 10 between what Warhol was doing and what Marcel Duchamp had done. It was Duchamp who in 1914 broke the rules and outraged the art world when he began exhibiting his objets trouvés, the coatstands, bottle racks, and bicycle wheels. Duchamp, critics suggested, had shown Warhol that appropriating common consumer items could be art.

Warhol was a particularly culpable pioneer of cultural nihilism 11 because the silkscreened readymades—soup cans, bottles, and such—were perceived to be the apotheoses of the objets trouvés.

So why is Warhol the most controversial artist of the century? 12 Read on:

Warhol's Place in Modernism

As a study of the criticism makes clear, Warhol appalled the art 13 establishment because he represented a complete transvaluation of the aesthetic principles that had dominated for several generations. What for years modernists had deliberately ignored or contemptuously spurned, Warhol embraced. As appropriated mass-culture images-such as his *Turquoise Marilyn* (1962)—his "art" was indistinguishable from advertising—meaning it was crass and pedestrian—and thus lampooned the modern emphasis on noble sentiment and good taste. No doubt Warhol's comments about art, that it should be effortless, that it's a business having nothing to do with transcendence, truth, or sentiment, also infuriated detractors.

Both Warhol's subject matter and his flippant attitudes toward 14 the conventions of the art world were the antithesis of the high-seriousness of modernism. And the rub of it was that his celebrations of the inconsequential were being taken seriously. It was a nasty slap in the face for those seeped in the myths of modernism.

Warhol's aesthetic contributed to the breakdown of the hierar- 15 chial conventions of modernism, dissolving distinctions between commercial design and serious art and the boundaries between popular taste and high culture—or, as some would have it, between trash and excellence.

Warhol and Postmodernism

As many observers now agree, the early 1960s mark the begin- 16 nings of a postmodern sensibility, where the modernist desire for closure and aesthetic autonomy has been rapidly replaced with indeterminacy and eclecticism.

If that's true, Warhol's art forecast and then highlighted the 17 changes that were occurring. And it has been argued that his art anticipated many ploys of this aesthetic new world, including the emphasis on irony, appropriation, and commonism, as well as promoting intellectual engagement through negation.

So What's Warhol's Place in the Criticism?

> *"Criticism is so old fashioned. Why don't you just put in a lot of gossip?"*
>
> —Warhol to Bob Colacello,
> longtime editor of Warhol's magazine *Interview*

In reviewing the critical record, one can conclude that Warhol's 18 role in art history is as a transitional figure. Stylistically his work is a bellwether, and the critical issues raised about him often converge with those at the center of the modern/postmodern debate. As a "mirror of the times," Warhol criticism reflects the trepidation and enthusiasm in response to shifting paradigms. Lucy Lippard's proposition is still valid—Warhol's images are ambiguous. It's this ambiguity that gives his work its edge. His images function as a sort of cultural Rorschach blot allowing for the projection of personalities, theoretical orientations, and ideological biases.

Why put fifty Cambell's soup cans on canvas? So far, there are scores of explanations. And the debate rages on . . . [19]

THE GETTYSBURG ADDRESS

Gilbert Highet

Fourscore and seven years ago our fathers brought forth on this continent, a new nation, conceived in Liberty, and dedicated to the proposition that all men are created equal.

Now we are engaged in a great civil war, testing whether that nation or any nation so conceived and so dedicated, can long endure. We are met on a great battle-field of that war. We have come to dedicate a portion of that field, as a final resting place for those who here gave their lives that that nation might live. It is altogether fitting and proper that we should do this.

But, in a larger sense, we can not dedicate—we can not consecrate—we can not hallow—this ground. The brave men, living and dead, who struggled here, have consecrated it, far above our poor power to add or detract. The world will little note, nor long remember, what we say here, but it can never forget what they did here. It is for us the living, rather, to be dedicated here to the unfinished work which they who fought here have thus far so nobly advanced. It is rather for us to be here dedicated to the great task remaining before us—that from these honored dead we take increased devotion to that cause for which they gave the last full measure of devotion—that we here highly resolve that these dead shall not have died in vain—that this nation, under God, shall have a new birth of freedom—and that government of the people, by the people, for the people, shall not perish from the earth.

Fourscore and seven years ago . . .   1

These five words stand at the entrance to the best-known monu-   2
ment of American prose, one of the finest utterances in the entire language and surely one of the greatest speeches in all history. Greatness is like granite: it is molded in fire, and it lasts for many centuries.

Fourscore and seven years ago. . . . It is strange to think that   3
President Lincoln was looking back to the 4th of July 1776, and that he and his speech are now further removed from us than he himself was from George Washington and the Declaration of Independence. Fourscore and seven years before the Gettysburg Address, a small group of patriots signed the Declaration. Fourscore and seven years after the Gettysburg Address, it was the year 1950, and that date is already receding rapidly into our troubled, adventurous, and valiant past.

Inadequately prepared and at first scarcely realized in its full importance, the dedication of the graveyard at Gettysburg was one of the supreme moments of American history. The battle itself had been a turning point of the war. On the 4th of July 1863, General Meade repelled Lee's invasion of Pennsylvania. Although he did not follow up his victory, he had broken one of the most formidable aggressive enterprises of the Confederate armies. Losses were heavy on both sides. Thousands of dead were left on the field, and thousands of wounded died in the hot days following the battle. At first, their burial was more or less haphazard; but thoughtful men gradually came to feel that an adequate burying place and memorial were required. These were established by an interstate commission that autumn, and the finest speaker in the North was invited to dedicate them. This was the scholar and statesman Edward Everett of Harvard. He made a good speech—which is still extant: not at all academic, it is full of close strategic analysis and deep historical understanding.

Lincoln was not invited to speak, at first. Although people knew him as an effective debater, they were not sure whether he was capable of making a serious speech on such a solemn occasion. But one of the impressive things about Lincoln's career is that he constantly strove to *grow*. He was anxious to appear on that occasion and to say something worthy of it. (Also, it has been suggested, he was anxious to remove the impression that he did not know how to behave properly—an impression which had been strengthened by a shocking story about his clowning on the battlefield of Antietam the previous year). Therefore when he was invited he took considerable care with his speech. He drafted rather more than half of it in the White House before leaving, finished it in the hotel at Gettysburg the night before the ceremony (not in the train, as sometimes reported), and wrote out a fair copy next morning.

There are many accounts of the day itself, 19 November 1863. There are many descriptions of Lincoln, all showing the same curious blend of grandeur and awkwardness, or lack of dignity, or—it would be best to call it humility. In the procession he rode horseback: a tall lean man in a high plug hat, straddling a short horse, with his feet too near the ground. He arrived before the chief speaker, and had to wait patiently for half an hour or more. His own speech came right at the end of a long and exhausting ceremony, lasted less than three minutes, and made little impression on the audience. In part this was because they were tired, in part because (as eyewitnesses said) he ended almost before they knew he had begun, and in part because he did not speak the Address, but read it, very slowly, in a thin high voice, with a marked Kentucky accent, pronouncing "to" as "toe" and dropping his final R's.

Some people of course were alert enough to be impressed. 7 Everett congratulated him at once. But most of the newspapers paid little attention to the speech, and some sneered at it. *The Patriot and Union* of Harrisburg wrote, "We pass over the silly remarks of the President; for the credit of the nation we are willing . . . that they shall no more be repeated or thought of"; and the London *Times* said, "The ceremony was rendered ludicrous by some of the sallies of that poor President Lincoln," calling his remarks "dull and commonplace." The first commendation of the Address came in a single sentence of the Chicago *Tribune*, and the first discriminating and detailed praise of it appeared in the Springfield *Republican*, the Providence *Journal*, and the Philadelphia *Bulletin*. However, three weeks after the ceremony and then again the following spring, the editor of *Harper's Weekly* published a sincere and thorough eulogy of the Address, and soon it was attaining recognition as a masterpiece.

> At the time, Lincoln could not care much about the reception of his words. He was exhausted and ill. In the train back to Washington, he lay down with a wet towel on his head. He had caught small-pox. At that moment he was incubating it, and he was stricken down soon after he reentered the White House. Fortunately it was a mild attack, and it evoked one of his best jokes: he told his visitors, "At last I have something I can give to everybody."

He had more than that to give to everybody. He was a unique 8 person, far greater than most people realize until they read his life with care. The wisdom of his policy, the sources of his statesmanship—these were things too complex to be discussed in a brief essay. But we can say something about the Gettysburg Address as a work of art.

A work of art. Yes: for Lincoln was a literary artist, trained both 9 by others and by himself. The textbooks he used as a boy were full of difficult exercises and skillful devices in formal rhetoric, stressing the qualities he practiced in his own speaking: antithesis, parallelism, and verbal harmony. Then he read and reread many admirable models of thought and expression: the King James Bible, the essays of Bacon, the best plays of Shakespeare. His favorites were *Hamlet, Lear, Macbeth, Richard III*, and *Henry VIII*, which he had read dozens of times. He loved reading aloud, too, and spent hours reading poetry to his friends. (He told his partner Herndon that he preferred getting the sense of any document by reading it aloud.) Therefore his serious speeches are important parts of the long and noble classical tradition of oratory which begins in Greece, runs through Rome to the modern world, and is still capable (if we do not neglect it) of producing masterpieces.

The first proof of this is that the Gettysburg Address is full of quotations—or rather of adaptations—which give it strength. It is partly religious, partly (in the highest sense) political: therefore it is interwoven with memories of the Bible and memories of American history. The first and the last words are Biblical cadences. Normally Lincoln did not say "fourscore" when he meant eighty but on this solemn occasion he recalled the important dates in the Bible—such as the age of Abram when his first son was born to him, and he was "fourscore and six years old."[1] Similarly he did not say there was a chance that democracy might die out: he recalled the somber phrasing of the Book of Job—where Bildad speaks of the destruction of one who shall vanish without a trace, and says that "his branch shall be cut off; his remembrance shall perish from the earth."[2] Then again, the famous description of our State as "government of the people, by the people, for the people" was adumbrated by Daniel Webster in 1830 (he spoke of "the people's government, made for the people, made by the people, and answerable to the people") and then elaborated in 1854 by the abolitionist Theodore Parker (as "government of all the people, by all the people, for all the people"). There is good reason to think that Lincoln took the important phrase "under God" (which he interpolated at the last moment) from Weems, the biographer of Washington; and we know that it had been used at least once by Washington himself.

Analyzing the Address further, we find that it is based on a highly imaginative theme, or group of themes. The subject is—how can we put it so as not to disfigure it?—the subject is the kinship of life and death, that mysterious linkage which we see sometimes as the physical succession of birth and death in our world, sometimes as the contrast, which is perhaps a unity, between death and immortality. The first sentence is concerned with birth:

Our *fathers brought forth a new* nation, *conceived* in liberty.

---

[1] "*Fourscore and six years old*": Genesis 16.16.

[2] "*his branch . . . earth*": Job 18.16–17.

The final phrase but one expresses the hope that

> this nation, under God, shall have a *new birth* of freedom.

And the last phrase of all speaks of continuing life as the triumph over death. Again and again throughout the speech, this mystical contrast and kinship reappear: "those who *gave their lives* that that nation might *live*," "the brave men *living* and *dead*," and so in the central assertion that the dead have already consecrated their own burial place, while "it is for us, the *living*, rather to be dedicated . . . to the great task remaining." The Gettysburg Address is a prose poem; it belongs to the same world as the great elegies, and the adagios of Beethoven. Its structure, however, is that of a skillfully contrived speech. The oratorical pattern is perfectly clear. Lincoln describes the occasion, dedicates the ground, and then draws a larger conclusion by calling on his hearers to dedicate themselves to the preservation of the Union. But within that, we can trace his constant use of at least two important rhetorical devices.

The first of these is *antithesis*: opposition, contrast. The speech is 12 full of it. Listen:

> The world will little *note*
> nor long *remember*   what *we say* here
> but it can never *forget*   what *they did* here.

And so in nearly every sentence: "brave men, *living* and *dead*"; "to *add* or *detract*." There is the antithesis of the Founding Fathers and the men of Lincoln's own time:

> Our *fathers brought forth* a new nation . . .
> now *we* are testing whether that nation . . . can *long endure*.

And there is the more terrible antithesis of those who have already died and those who still live to do their duty. Now, antithesis is the figure of contrast and conflict. Lincoln was speaking in the midst of a great civil war.

The other important pattern is different. It is technically called *tri-* 13 *colon*—the division of an idea into three harmonious parts, usually of increasing power. The most famous phrase of the Address is a tricolon:

> government of the people
>   by the people
>   and   for the people

The most solemn sentence is a tricolon:

> we cannot dedicate
> we cannot consecrate
> we cannot hallow this ground.

And above all, the last sentence (which has sometimes been criticized as too complex) is essentially two parallel phrases, with a tricolon growing out of the second and then producing another tricolon: a trunk, three branches, and a cluster of flowers. Lincoln says that it is for his hearers to be dedicated to the great task remaining before them. Then he goes on,

> that from these honored dead

—apparently he means "in such a way that from these honored dead"—

> we take increased devotion to that cause.

Next, he restates this more briefly:

> that we here highly resolve . . .

And now the actual resolution follows, in three parts of growing intensity:

> that these dead shall not have died in vain
> that this nation, under God, shall have a new birth of freedom

and that (one more tricolon)

> government of the people
>   by the people
>   and   for the people
> shall not perish from the earth.

Now, the tricolon is the figure which, through division, emphasizes basic harmony and unity. Lincoln used antithesis because he was speaking to a people at war. He used the tricolon because he was hoping, planning, praying for peace.

No one thinks that when he was drafting the Gettysburg 14
Address, Lincoln deliberately looked up these quotations and consciously chose these particular patterns of thought. No, he chose the
theme. From its development and from the emotional tone of the
entire occasion, all the rest followed, or grew—by that marvelous
process of choice and rejection which is essential to artistic creation.
It does not spoil such a work of art to analyze it as closely as we have
done; it is altogether fitting and proper that we should do this: for it
helps us to penetrate more deeply into the rich meaning of the
Gettysburg Address, and it allows us the very rare privilege of
watching the workings of a great man's mind.

6

PROBLEM SOLVING

IT'S EASY BEING GREEN

Bill McKibben

The more I surveyed my new car, the happier I got. "New car" is 1
one of those phrases that make Americans unreasonably happy to
begin with. And this one—well, it was a particularly shiny metallic
blue. Better yet, it was the first Honda Civic hybrid electric sold in the
state of Vermont: I'd traded in my old Civic (40 miles to the gallon),
and now the little screen behind the steering wheel was telling me
that I was getting 50, 51, 52 miles to the gallon. Even better yet, I was
doing nothing strange or difficult or conspicuously ecological. If you
didn't know there was an electric motor assisting the small gas
engine—well, you'd never know. The owner's manual devoted far
more space to the air bags and the heating system. It didn't look
goofily Jetsonish like Honda's first hybrid, the two-seater Insight
introduced in 2000. Instead, it looked like a Civic, the most vanilla car
ever produced. "Our goal was to make it look, for lack of a better
word, normal," explained Kevin Bynoe, spokesman for American
Honda.

And the happier I got, the angrier I got. Because, as the Honda 2
and a raft of other recent developments powerfully proved, energy
efficiency, energy conservation, and renewable energy are ready for
prime time. No longer the niche province of incredibly noble backyard tinkerers distilling biodiesel from used vegetable oil or building
homes from Earth rammed into tires, the equipment and attitudes
necessary to radically transform our energy system are now main-
stream enough for those of us too lazy or too busy to try anything
that seems hard. And yet the switch toward sensible energy still isn't
happening. A few weeks before I picked up my car, an overwhelm-

ing bipartisan vote in the Senate had rejected calls to increase the mileage of the nation's new car fleet by 2015—to increase it to 36 mpg, not as good as the Civic I'd traded in to buy this hybrid. The administration was pressing ahead with its plan for more drilling and refining. The world was suffering the warmest winter in history as more carbon dioxide pushed global temperatures ever higher. And people were dying in conflicts across wide swaths of the world, the casualties—at least in some measure—of America's insatiable demand for energy.

In other words, the gap between what we could be doing and ³ what we are doing has never been wider. Consider:

- The Honda I was driving was the third hybrid model easily available in this country, following in the tire tracks of the Insight and the Toyota Prius. They take regular gas, they require nothing in the way of special service, and they boast waiting lists. And yet Detroit, despite a decade of massive funding from the Clinton administration, can't sell you one. Instead, after September 11, the automakers launched a massive campaign (zero financing, red, white, and blue ads) to sell existing stock, particularly the gas-sucking SUVs that should by all rights come with their own little Saudi flags on the hood.

- Even greater boosts in efficiency can come when you build or renovate a home. Alex Wilson, editor of *Environmental Building News*, says the average American house may be 20 percent more energy efficient than it was two decades ago, but simple tweaks like better windows and bulkier insulation could save 30 to 50 percent more energy with "very little cost implication." And yet building codes do almost nothing to boost such technologies, and the Bush administration is fighting to roll back efficiency gains for some appliances that Clinton managed to push through. For instance, air-conditioner manufacturers recently won a battle in the Senate to let them get away with making their machines only 20 percent more efficient, not the 30 percent current law demands. The difference in real terms? Sixty new power plants across the country by 2030.

- Or consider electric generation. For a decade or two, environmentalists had their fingers crossed when they talked about renewables. It was hard to imagine most Americans really trading in their grid connection for backyard solar panels with their finicky batteries. But such trade-offs are less necessary by the day. Around the world, wind power is growing more quickly than any other form of energy—Denmark, Germany, Spain, and India all generate big amounts of their power from ultra-modern wind turbines. But in this country, where the never-ending breeze across the High Plains could generate twice as much electricity as the country uses, progress has been extraordinarily slow. (North Dakota, the windiest state in the union, has exactly four turbines.) Wind power is finally beginning to get some serious attention from the energy industry, but the technology won't live up to its potentia! until politicians stop subsidizing fossil fuels and give serious boosts to the alternatives.

And not all those politicians are conservative, either. In 4 Massachusetts, even some true progressives, like the gubernatorial candidate Robert Reich, can't bring themselves to endorse a big wind installation proposed for six miles off Cape Cod. They have lots of arguments, most of which boil down to NIVOMD (Not in View of My Deck), a position particularly incongruous since Cape Cod will sink quickly beneath the Atlantic unless every weapon in the fight against global warming is employed as rapidly as possible.

What really haunts energy experts is the sense that, for the first 5 time since the oil shocks of the early 1970s, the nation could have rallied around the cause of energy conservation and renewable alternatives last fall. In the wake of September 11, they agree, the president could have announced a pair of national goals—capture Osama and free ourselves from the oil addiction that leaves us endlessly vulnerable. "President Bush's failure will haunt me for decades," says Alan Durning, president of Northwest Environment Watch. "Bush had a chance to advance, in a single blow, three pressing national priorities: national security, economic recovery, and environmental protection. All the stars were aligned." If only, says Brent Blackwelder, president of Friends of the Earth, Bush had set a goal, like JFK and the space program. "We could totally get off oil in three decades." Instead, the president used the crisis to push for drilling in the Arctic National Wildlife Refuge, a present to campaign contributors that would yield a statistically insignificant new supply ten years down the road.

It's not just new technologies that Bush could have pushed, of 6 course. Americans were, at least for a little while, in the mood to do something, to make some sacrifice, to rally around some cause. In the words of Charles Komanoff, a New York energy analyst, "The choice is between love of oil and love of country," and at least "in the initial weeks after September 11, it seemed that Americans were awakening at last to the true cost of their addiction to oil." In an effort to take

advantage of that political window, Komanoff published a booklet
showing just how simple it would be to cut America's oil use by 5 or
10 percent—not over the years it will take for the new technologies to
really kick in, but over the course of a few weeks and with only
minor modifications to our way of life.

For instance, he calculated, we could save 7 percent of the gaso-   7
line we use simply by eliminating one car trip in fourteen. The little
bit of planning required to make sure you visit the grocery store three
times a week instead of four would leave us with endlessly more oil
than sucking dry the Arctic. Indeed, Americans are so energy-profli-
gate that even minor switches save significant sums—if half the dri-
vers in two-car households switched just a tenth of their travel to
their more efficient vehicle, we'd instantly save 1 percent of our oil.
Keep the damn Explorer; just leave it in the driveway once a week
and drive the Camry.

A similar menu of small changes—cutting back on one airplane   8
trip in seven, turning down the thermostat two degrees, screwing in
a few compact fluorescent bulbs—and all of a sudden our endlessly
climbing energy usage begins to decline. Impossible? Americans
won't do it? Look at California. With the threat of power shortages
looming and with some clever incentives provided by government
and utilities, Californians last year found an awful lot of small ways
to save energy that really added up: 79 percent reported taking some
steps, and a third of households managed to cut their electric use by
more than 20 percent. Not by becoming a Third World nation (the
state's economy continued to grow), not by living in caves, not by
suffering—but by turning off the lights when they left the room. In
just the first six months of 2001, the Colorado energy guru Amory
Lovins pointed out recently, "customers wiped out California's previous five to ten years of demand growth." Now the same companies
that were scrambling to build new plants for the Golden State a year
ago are backing away from their proposals, spooked by the possibility of an energy glut.

It's only in Washington, in fact, that nobody gets it. If you go to   9
Europe or Asia, you'll find nations increasingly involved in planning
for a different energy future: Every industrial country but the United
States signed on to the Kyoto agreement at the last international conference on global warming, and some of those nations may actually
meet their targets for carbon dioxide reductions. The Dutch consumer demand for green power outstrips even the capacity of their
growing wind farms, while the Germans have taken the logical step

of raising taxes on carbon-based fuels and eliminating them on renewable sources. Reducing fossil fuel use is an accepted, inevitable part of the political process on the Continent, the same way that "fighting crime" is in this country, and Europeans look with growing disgust at the depth of our addiction—only the events of September 11 saved America from a wave of universal scorn when Bush backed away from the Kyoto pact.

And in state capitols and city halls around this country, local 10 leaders are beginning to act as well. Voters in San Francisco last year overwhelmingly approved an initiative to require municipal purchases of solar and wind power; in Seattle, the mayor's office announced an ambitions plan to meet or beat the Kyoto targets within the confines of the city and four suburbs.

Perhaps such actions might be expected in San Francisco and 11 Seattle. But in June of 2001, the Chicago city government signed a contract with Commonwealth Edison to buy 10 percent of its power from renewables, a figure due to increase to 20 percent in five years. And in Salt Lake City, of all places, Mayor Rocky Anderson announced on the opening day of the Winter Olympics that his city, too, was going to meet the Kyoto standards—already, in fact, crews were at work changing lightbulbs in street lamps and planning new mass transit.

Even many big American corporations have gone much further than the Bush administration. As Alex Wilson, the green building 12 expert, points out, "Corporations are pretty good at looking at the bottom line, which is directly affected by operating costs. They're good with numbers." If you can make your product with half the energy, well, that's just as good as increasing sales—and if you can put a windmill on the cover of your annual report, that's gravy.

In short, what pretty much everyone outside the White House has realized is this: The great economic shift of this century will be 13 away from fossil fuels and toward renewable energy. That shift will happen with or without George W. Bush—there are too many reasons, from environmental to economic to geopolitical necessity, for it not to. But American policy can slow down the transition, perhaps by decades, and that is precisely what the administration would like to see. They have two reasons: One is the enormous debt they owe to the backers of their political careers, those coal and oil and gas guys who dictated large sections of the new energy policy. Those industries want to wring every last penny from their mines, their drill rigs, and their refineries—and if those extra decades mean that the planet's temperature rises a few degrees, well, that's business.

The other reason is just as powerful, though—it's the fear that 14
Americans will blame their leaders if prices for gas go up too quickly.
It's not an idle fear—certainly it was shared by Bill Clinton, who did
nothing to stem the nation's love affair with SUVs, and by Al Gore,
who, during his presidential campaign, demanded that the Strategic
Petroleum Reserve be opened to drive down prices at the pump. But
that's what makes Bush's post-September silence on this issue so sad.
For once a U.S. president had the chance to turn it all around—to say
that this was a sacrifice we needed to make and one that any patriot
would support. It's tragically likely he will have the same opportunity
again in the years ahead, and tragically unlikely that he will take it.

In the meantime, there's work to be done in statehouses and city 15
halls. And at the car lot—at least the ones with the Honda and Toyota
signs out front. "This Civic has a slightly different front end and a
roof-mounted antenna," says Honda's Bynoe. "But other than that, it
looks like a regular Civic, and it drives like one too. It's not necessarily for hard-core enviros. You don't have to scream about it at the top
of your lungs. It's just a car." But a very shiny blue. And I just came
back from a trip to Boston: 59 miles to the gallon.

ON WRITING

Stephen King

If you want to be a writer, you must do two things above all oth- 1
ers: read a lot and write a lot. There's no way around these two things
that I'm aware of, no shortcut.

I'm a slow reader, but I usually get through seventy or eighty 2
books a year, mostly fiction. I don't read in order to study the craft; I
read because I like to read. It's what I do at night, kicked back in my
blue chair. Similarly, I don't read fiction to study the art of fiction, but
simply because I like stories. Yet there is a learning process going on.
Every book you pick up has its own lesson or lessons, and quite often
the bad books have more to teach than the good ones.

When I was in the eighth grade, I happened upon a paperback 3
novel by Murray Leinster, a science fiction pulp writer who did most
of his work during the forties and fifties, when magazines like
Amazing Stories paid a penny a word. I had read other books by Mr.
Leinster, enough to know that the quality of his writing was uneven.
This particular tale, which was about mining in the asteroid belt, was
one of his less successful efforts. Only that's too kind. It was terrible,
actually, a story populated by paper-thin characters and driven by
outlandish plot developments. Worst of all (or so it seemed to me at
the time), Leinster had fallen in love with the word *zestful*.

Characters watched the approach of ore-bearing asteroids with 4
zestful smiles. Characters sat down to supper aboard their mining ship
with *zestful anticipation*. Near the end of the book, the hero swept the
large-breasted, blonde heroine into a *zestful embrace*. For me, it was
the literary equivalent of a smallpox vaccination: I have never, so far
as I know, used the word *zestful* in a novel or a story. God willing, I
never will.

Asteroid Miners (which wasn't the title, but that's close enough) 5
was an important book in my life as a reader. Almost everyone can
remember losing his or her virginity, and most writers can remember
the first book he/she put down thinking: *I can do better than this. Hell,
I am doing better than this!* What could be more encouraging to the
struggling writer than to realize his/her work is unquestionably better than that of someone who actually got paid for his/her stuff?

One learns most clearly what not to do by reading bad prose— 6
one novel like *Asteroid Miners* (or *Valley of the Dolls*, *Flowers in the
Attic*, and *The Bridges of Madison County*, to name just a few) is worth

a semester at a good writing school, even with the superstar guest lecturers thrown in.

Good writing, on the other hand, teaches the learning writer 7 about style, graceful narration, plot development, the creation of believable characters, and truth-telling. A novel like *The Grapes of Wrath* may fill a new writer with feelings of despair and good old-fashioned jealousy—"I'll never be able to write anything that good, not if I live to be a thousand"—but such feelings can also serve as a spur, goading the writer to work harder and aim higher. Being swept away by a combination of great story and great writing—of being flattened, in fact—is part of every writer's necessary formation. You cannot hope to sweep someone else away by the force of your writing until it has been done to you.

So we read to experience the mediocre and the outright rotten; 8 such experience helps us to recognize those things when they begin to creep into our own work, and to steer clear of them. We also read in order to measure ourselves against the good and the great, to get a sense of all that can be done. And we read in order to experience different styles.

You may find yourself adopting a style you find particularly 9 exciting, and there's nothing wrong with that. When I read Ray Bradbury as a kid, I wrote like Ray Bradbury—everything green and wondrous and seen through a lens smeared with the grease of nostalgia. When I read James M. Cain, everything I wrote came out clipped and stripped and hard-boiled. When I read Lovecraft, my prose became luxurious and Byzantine. I wrote stories in my teenage years where all these styles merged, creating a kind of hilarious stew. This sort of stylistic blending is a necessary part of developing one's own style, but it doesn't occur in a vacuum. You have to read widely, constantly refining (and redefining) your own work as you do so. It's hard for me to believe that people who read very little (or not at all in some cases) should presume to write and expect people to like what they have written, but I know it's true. If I had a nickel for every person who ever told me he/she wanted to become a writer but "didn't have time to read," I could buy myself a pretty good steak dinner. Can I be blunt on this subject? If you don't have time to read, you don't have the time (or the tools) to write. Simple as that.

Reading is the creative center of a writer's life. I take a book with 10 me everywhere I go, and find there are all sorts of opportunities to dip in. The trick is to teach yourself to read in small sips as well as in long swallows. Waiting rooms were made for books—of course! But so are theater lobbies before the show, long and boring checkout lines, and everyone's favorite, the john. You can even read while you're driving, thanks to the audiobook revolution. Of the books I read each year, anywhere from six to a dozen are on tape. As for all the wonderful radio you will be missing, come on—how many times can you listen to Deep Purple sing "Highway Star"?

Reading at meals is considered rude in polite society, but if you expect to succeed as a writer, rudeness should be the second-to-least of your concerns. The least of all should be polite society and what it expects. If you intend to write as truthfully as you can, your days as a member of polite society are numbered, anyway.

Where else can you read? There's always the treadmill, or whatever you use down at the local health club to get aerobic. I try to spend an hour doing that every day, and I think I'd go mad without a good novel to keep me company. Most exercise facilities (at home as well as outside it) are now equipped with TVs, but TV—while working out or anywhere else—really is about the last thing an aspiring writer needs. If you feel you must have the news analyst blowhards on CNN while you exercise, or the stock market blowhards on MSNBC, or the sports blowhards on ESPN, it's time for you to question how serious you really are about becoming a writer. You must be prepared to do some serious turning inward toward the life of the imagination, and that means, I'm afraid, that Geraldo, Keith Obermann, and Jay Leno must go. Reading takes time, and the glass teat takes too much of it.

Once weaned from the ephemeral craving for TV, most people will find they enjoy the time they spend reading. I'd like to suggest that turning off that endlessly quacking box is apt to improve the quality of your life as well as the quality of your writing. And how much of a sacrifice are we talking about here? How many *Frasier* and *ER* reruns does it take to make one American life complete? How many Richard Simmons infomercials? How many whiteboy/fatboy Beltway insiders on CNN? Oh man, don't get me started. Jerry-Springer-Dr.-Dre-Judge-Judy-Jerry-Falwell-Donny-and-Marie, I rest my case.

When my son Owen was seven or so, he fell in love with Bruce Springsteen's E Street Band, particularly with Clarence Clemons, the band's burly sax player. Owen decided he wanted to learn to play like Clarence. My wife and I were amused and delighted by this ambition. We were also hopeful, as any parent would be, that our kid would turn out to be talented, perhaps even some sort of prodigy. We got Owen a tenor saxophone for Christmas and lessons with Gordon Bowie, one of the local music men. Then we crossed our fingers and hoped for the best.

Seven months later I suggested to my wife that it was time to dis- 15 continue the sax lessons, if Owen concurred. Owen did, and with palpable relief—he hadn't wanted to say it himself, especially not after asking for the sax in the first place, but seven months had been long enough for him to realize that, while he might love Clarence Clemons's big sound, the saxophone was simply not for him—God had not given him that particular talent.

I knew, not because Owen stopped practicing, but because he 16 was practicing only during the periods Mr. Bowie had set for him: half an hour after school four days a week, plus an hour on the week-ends. Owen mastered the scales and the notes—nothing wrong with his memory, his lungs, or his eye-hand coordination—but we never heard him taking off, surprising himself with something new, bliss-ing himself out. And as soon as his practice time was over, it was back into the case with the horn, and there it stayed until the next les-son or practice-time. What this suggested to me was that when it came to the sax and my son, there was never going to be any real play-time; it was all going to be rehearsal. That's no good. If there's no joy in it, it's just no good. It's best to go on to some other area, where the deposits of talent may be richer and the fun quotient higher.

Talent renders the whole idea of rehearsal meaningless; when 17 you find something at which you are talented, you do it (whatever *it* is) until your fingers bleed or your eyes are ready to fall out of your head. Even when no one is listening (or reading, or watching), every outing is a bravura performance, because you as the creator are happy. Perhaps even ecstatic. That goes for reading and writing as well as for playing a musical instrument, hitting a baseball, or run-ning the four-forty. The sort of strenuous reading and writing pro-gram I advocate—four to six hours a day, every day—will not seem strenuous if you really enjoy doing these things and have an aptitude for them; in fact, you may be following such a program already. If you feel you need permission to do all the reading and writing your little heart desires, however, consider it hereby granted by yours truly.

The real importance of reading is that it creates an ease and inti- 18 macy with the process of writing; one comes to the country of the writer with one's papers and identification pretty much in order. Constant reading will pull you into a place (a mind-set, if you like the phrase) where you can write eagerly and without self-consciousness. It also offers you a constantly growing knowledge of what has been done and what hasn't, what is trite and what is fresh, what works and what just lies there dying (or dead) on the page. The more you read, the less apt you are to make a fool of yourself with your pen or word processor.

A MODEST PROPOSAL

Jonathan Swift

For Preventing the Children of
Poor People in Ireland from Being a Burden to
Their Parents or Country, and for Making
Them Beneficial to the Public

It is a melancholy object to those who walk through this great 1
town,[1] or travel in the country, when they see the streets, the roads,
and cabin doors crowded with beggars of the female sex, followed by
three, four, or six children, all in rags and importuning every passenger for an alms. These mothers, instead of being able to work for their
honest livelihood, are forced to employ all their time in strolling to
beg sustenance for their helpless infants; who as they grow up either
turn thieves, for want of work, or leave their dear native country to
fight for the Pretender[2] in Spain, or sell themselves to the Barbados.[3]

I think it is agreed by all parties that this prodigious number of 2
children in the arms, or on the backs, or at the heels of their mothers,
and frequently of their fathers, is, in the present deplorable state of
the kingdom, a very great additional grievance; and therefore who-
ever could find out a fair, cheap, and easy method of making these
children sound, useful members of the commonwealth would
deserve so well of the public as to have his statue set up for a pre-
server of the nation.

But my intention is very far from being confined to provide only 3
for the children of professed beggars: it is of a much greater extent
and shall take in the whole number of infants at a certain age who are
born of parents in effect as little able to support them as those who
demand our charity in the streets.

As to my own part, having turned my thoughts for many years 4
upon this important subject and maturely weighed the several
schemes of other projectors, I have always found them grossly mis-

---

[1] *this great town:* Dublin.

[2] *the Pretender:* James Stuart (1688–1766), son of King James II, "pretender" or claimant to the
throne which his father had lost in the Revolution of 1688. He was Catholic, and Ireland was
loyal to him.

[3] *sell . . . Barbados:* Because of extreme poverty, many of the Irish bound or sold themselves to
obtain passage to the West Indies or other British possessions in North America. They agreed to
work for their new masters, usually planters, for a specified number of years.

taken in their computation. It is true, a child just dropped from its dam may be supported by her milk for a solar year, with little other nourishment: at most not above the value of two shillings, which the mother may certainly get, or the value in scraps, by her lawful occupation of begging; and it is exactly at one year old that I propose to provide for them in such a manner, as, instead of being a charge upon their parents or the parish, or wanting food and raiment for the rest of their lives, they shall, on the contrary, contribute to the feeding and partly to the clothing of many thousands.

There is likewise another great advantage in my scheme, that it will prevent those voluntary abortions and that horrid practice of women murdering their bastard children, alas! too frequent among us, sacrificing the poor innocent babes, I doubt more to avoid the expense than the shame, which would move tears and pity in the most savage and inhuman breast. 5

The number of souls in this kingdom being usually reckoned one million and a half, of these I calculate there may be about two hundred thousand couple whose wives are breeders; from which number I subtract thirty thousand couple; who are able to maintain their own children (although I apprehend there cannot be so many, under the present distresses of the kingdom), but this being granted, there will remain an hundred and seventy thousand breeders. I again subtract fifty thousand for those women who miscarry, or whose children die by accident or disease within the year. There only remain one hundred and twenty thousand children of poor parents annually born. The question therefore is, How this number shall be reared and provided for? which, as I have already said, under the present situation of affairs, is utterly impossible by all the methods hitherto proposed. For we can neither employ them in handicraft or agriculture; we neither build houses (I mean in the country) nor cultivate land: they can very seldom pick up a livelihood by stealing till they arrive at six years old, except where they are of towardly[4] parts; although I confess they learn the rudiments much earlier, during which time they can, however, be properly looked upon only as probationers; as I have been informed by a principal gentleman in the county of Cavan, who protested to me that he never knew above one or two instances under the age of six, even in a part of the kingdom so renowned for the quickest proficiency in that art. 6

---

[4] *towardly:* dutiful; easily managed.

I am assured by our merchants that a boy or a girl before twelve years old is no salable commodity; and even when they come to this age they will not yield above three pounds, or three pounds and half a crown at most, on the exchange; which cannot turn to account either to the parents or kingdom, the charge of nutriment and rags having been at least four times that value. [7]

I shall now therefore humbly propose my own thoughts, which I hope will not be liable to the least objection. [8]

I have been assured by a very knowing American of my acquaintance in London that a young healthy child well nursed is at a year old a most delicious, nourishing, and wholesome food, whether stewed, roasted, baked, or boiled; and I make no doubt that it will equally serve in a fricassee or a ragout.[5] [9]

I do therefore humbly offer it to public consideration that of the hundred and twenty thousand children already computed, twenty thousand may be reserved for breed, whereof only one-fourth part to be males; which is more than we allow to sheep, black cattle, or swine; and my reason is that these children are seldom the fruits of marriage, a circumstance not much regarded by our savages; therefore one male will be sufficient to serve four females. That the remaining hundred thousand may, at a year old, be offered in sale to the persons of quality and fortune through the kingdom; always advising the mother to let them suck plentifully in the last month, so as to render them plump and fat for a good table. A child will make two dishes at an entertainment for friends; and when the family dines alone, the fore or hind quarter will make a reasonable dish, and seasoned with a little pepper or salt will be very good boiled on the fourth day, especially in winter. [10]

I have reckoned upon a medium that a child just born will weigh twelve pounds, and in a solar year, if tolerably nursed, will increase to twenty-eight pounds. [11]

I grant this food will be somewhat dear, and therefore very proper for landlords, who, as they have already devoured most of the parents, seem to have the best title to the children. [12]

Infant's flesh will be in season throughout the year, but more plentifully in March, and a little before and after for we are told by a grave author, an eminent French physician,[6] that fish being a prolific [13]

---

[5] *ragout:* (ra gü), a highly seasoned meat stew.

[6] *grave author . . . physician:* François Rabelais (c. 1494–1553), who was anything but a "grave author."

diet, there are more children born in Roman Catholic countries about nine months after Lent than at any other season; therefore, reckoning a year after Lent, the markets will be more glutted than usual, because the number of popish infants is at least three to one in this kingdom: and therefore it will have one other collateral advantage, by lessening the number of papists among us.

I have already computed the charge of nursing a beggar's child 14 (in which list I reckon all cottagers, laborers, and four-fifths of the farmers) to be about two shillings per annum, rags included; and I believe no gentleman would repine to give ten shillings for the carcass of a good fat child, which, as I have said, will make four dishes of excellent nutritive meat, when he has only some particular friend or his own family to dine with him. Thus the squire will learn to be a good landlord and grow popular among his tenants; the mother will have eight shillings net profit and be fit for work till she produces another child.

Those who are more thrifty (as I must confess the times require) 15 may flay the carcass; the skin of which artificially[7] dressed will make admirable gloves for ladies and summer boots for fine gentlemen.

As to our city of Dublin, shambles[8] may be appointed for this 16 purpose in the most convenient parts of it, and butchers we may be assured will not be wanting; although I rather recommend buying the children alive and dressing them hot from the knife as we do roasting pigs.

A very worthy person, a true lover of his country, and whose 17 virtues I highly esteem, was lately pleased, in discoursing on this matter, to offer a refinement upon my scheme. He said that many gentlemen of this kingdom, having of late destroyed their deer, he conceived that the want of venison might be well supplied by the bodies of young lads and maidens, not exceeding fourteen years of age nor under twelve; so great a number of both sexes in every country being now ready to starve for want of work and service; and these to be disposed of by their parents, if alive, or otherwise by their nearest relations. But with due deference to so excellent a friend and so deserving a patriot, I cannot be altogether in his sentiments; for as to the males, my American acquaintance assured me from frequent experience that their flesh was generally tough and lean, like that of our schoolboys, by continual exercise, and their taste disagreeable;

---

[7] *artificially:* artfully; skillfully.
[8] *shambles:* slaughterhouses.

and to fatten them would not answer the charge. Then as to the females, it would, I think, with humble submission be a loss to the public, because they soon would become breeders themselves: and besides, it is not improbable that some scrupulous people might be apt to censure such a practice (although indeed very unjustly), as a little bordering upon cruelty; which, I confess, has always been with me the strongest objection against any project, how well soever intended.

But in order to justify my friend, he confessed that this expedient 18 was put into his head by the famous Psalmanazar,[9] a native of the island Formosa, who came from thence to London above twenty years ago: and in conversation told my friend that in his country when any young person happened to be put to death, the executioner sold the carcass to persons of quality as a prime dainty; and that in his time the body of a plump girl of fifteen, who was crucified for an attempt to poison the emperor, was sold to his imperial majesty's prime minister of state, and other great mandarins of the court, in joints from the gibbet, at four hundred crowns. Neither indeed can I deny that if the same use were made of several plump girls in this town, who, without one single groat to their fortunes, cannot stir abroad without a chair, and appear at a playhouse and assemblies in foreign fineries which they never will pay for, the kingdom would not be the worse.

Some persons of a desponding spirit are in great concern about 19 that vast number of poor people who are aged, diseased, or maimed; and I have been desired to employ my thoughts, what course may be taken to ease the nation of so grievous an encumbrance. But I am not in the least pain upon that matter, because it is very well known that they are every day dying and rotting, by cold and famine, and filth and vermin, as fast as can be reasonably expected. And as to the young laborers, they are now in almost as hopeful a condition: they cannot get work, and consequently pine away for want of nourishment to a degree that if at any time they are accidentally hired to common labor, they have not strength to perform it; and thus the country and themselves are happily delivered from the evils to come.

---

[9] *Psalmanazar:* the imposter George Psalmanazar (c. 1679–1763), a Frenchman who passed himself off in England as a Formosan, and wrote a totally fictional "true" account of Formosa, in which he described cannibalism.

I have too long digressed and therefore shall return to my sub- 20
ject. I think the advantages, by the proposal which I have made, are
obvious and many, as well as of the highest importance.

For first, as I have already observed, it would greatly lessen the 21
number of papists, with whom we are yearly overrun, being the principal breeders of the nation, as well as our most dangerous enemies;
and who stay at home on purpose to deliver the kingdom to the
Pretender, hoping to take their advantage by the absence of so many
good Protestants, who have chosen rather to leave their country than
stay at home and pay tithes against their conscience to an Episcopal
curate.[10]

Secondly, the poorer tenants will have something valuable of 22
their own, which by law may be made liable to distress,[11] and help to
pay their landlord's rent; their corn and cattle being already seized,
and money a thing unknown.

Thirdly, whereas the maintenance of a hundred thousand chil- 23
dren, from two years old and upwards, cannot be computed at less
than ten shillings a piece per annum, the nation's stock will be
thereby increased fifty thousand pounds per annum, beside the
profit of a new dish introduced to the tables of all gentlemen of fortune in the kingdom who have any refinement in taste. And the
money will circulate among ourselves, the goods being entirely of
our own growth and manufacture.

Fourthly, the constant breeders, besides the gain of eight shillings 24
sterling per annum by the sale of their children, will be rid of the
charge of maintaining them after the first year.

Fifthly, this food would likewise bring great custom to taverns: 25
where the vintners will certainly be so prudent as to procure the best
receipts for dressing it to perfection, and consequently have their
houses frequented by all the fine gentlemen, who justly value themselves upon their knowledge in good eating and a skilful cook, who
understands how to oblige his guests, will contrive to make it as
expensive as they please.

Sixthly, this would be a great inducement to marriage, which all 26
wise nations have either encouraged by rewards or enforced by laws
and penalties. It would increase the care and tenderness of mothers
toward their children, when they were sure of a settlement for life to
the poor babes, provided in some sort by the public, to their annual

---

[10] *Protestants . . . curate:* Swift is here attacking the absentee landlords.

[11] *distress:* distraint, the legal seizure of property for payment of debts.

profit instead of expense. We should see an honest emulation among the married women, which of them could bring the fattest child to the market. Men would become as fond of their wives during the time of their pregnancy as they are now of their mares in foal, their cows in calf, or sows when they are ready to farrow; nor offer to beat or kick them (as is too frequent a practice) for fear of a miscarriage.

Many other advantages might be enumerated. For instance, the addition of some thousand carcasses in our exportation of barreled beef, the propagation of swine's flesh, and improvement in the art of making good bacon, so much wanted among us by the great destruction of pigs, too frequent at our tables; which are no way comparable in taste or magnificence to a well grown, fat, yearling child, which roasted whole will make a considerable figure at a lord mayor's feast, or any other public entertainment. But this and many others I omit, being studious of brevity.   27

Supposing that one thousand families in this city would be constant customers for infants' flesh, besides others who might have it at merry meetings, particularly weddings and christenings, I compute that Dublin would take off annually about twenty thousand carcasses; and the rest of the kingdom (where probably they will be sold somewhat cheaper) the remaining eighty thousand.   28

I can think of no one objection that will possibly be raised against this proposal, unless it should be urged that the number of people will be thereby much lessened in the kingdom. This I freely own, and it was indeed one principal design in offering it to the world. I desire the reader will observe that I calculate my remedy for this one individual kingdom of Ireland, and for no other that ever was, is, or, I think, ever can be upon earth. Therefore let no man talk to me of other expedients: of taxing our absentees at five shillings a pound: of using neither clothes nor household furniture, except what is of our own growth and manufacture: of utterly rejecting the materials and instruments that promote foreign luxury: of curing the expensiveness of pride, vanity, idleness, and gaming in our women of introducing a vein of parsimony, prudence, and temperance: of learning to love our country, in the want of which we differ even from Laplanders and the inhabitants of Topinamboo:[12] of quitting our animosities and factions, nor acting any longer like the Jews, who were murdering one   29

---

[12] *Topinamboo:* a savage area of Brazil.

another at the very moment their city was taken:[13] of being a little cautious not to sell our country and conscience for nothing: of teaching landlords to have at least one degree of mercy toward their tenants: lastly, of putting a spirit of honesty, industry, and skill into our shopkeepers; who, if a resolution could now be taken to buy only our native goods, would immediately unite to cheat and exact upon us in the price, the measure, and the goodness, nor could ever yet be brought to make one fair proposal of just dealing, though often and earnestly invited to it.[14]

Therefore, I repeat, let no man talk to me of these and the like 30 expedients, till he has at least some glimpse of hope that there will ever be some hearty and sincere attempt to put them in practice.

But as to myself, having been wearied out for many years with 31 offering vain, idle, visionary thoughts, and at length utterly despairing of success, I fortunately fell upon this proposal; which, as it is wholly new, so it has something solid and real, of no expense and little trouble, full in our own power, and whereby we can incur no danger in disobliging England. For this kind of commodity will not bear exportation, the flesh being of too tender a consistence to admit a long continuance in salt, although perhaps I could name a country which would be glad to eat up our whole nation without it.[15]

After all, I am not so violently bent upon my own opinion as to 32 reject any offer proposed by wise men, which shall be found equally innocent, cheap, easy, and effectual. But before something of that kind shall be advanced in contradiction to my scheme, and offering a better, I desire the author or authors will be pleased maturely to consider two points. First, as things now stand, how they will be able to find food and raiment for an hundred thousand useless mouths and backs. And, secondly, there being a round million of creatures in human figure throughout this kingdom, whose whole subsistence put into a common stock would leave them in debt two millions of pounds sterling, adding those who are beggars by profession to the bulk of farmers, cottagers, and laborers, with their wives and children, who are beggars in effect; I desire those politicians, who dislike

---

[13]*city was taken:* While the Roman Emperor Titus was besieging Jerusalem, which he took and destroyed in A.D. 70, within the city factions of fanatics were waging bloody warfare.

[14]*invited to it:* Swift had already made all these proposals in various pamphlets.

[15]*a country . . . without it:* England; this is another way of saying, "The English are devouring the Irish."

my overture, and may perhaps be so bold as to attempt an answer, that they will first ask the parents of these mortals, whether they would not at this day think it a great happiness to have been sold for food at a year old in the manner I prescribe, and thereby have avoided such a perpetual scene of misfortunes as they have since gone through by the oppression of landlords, the impossibility of paying rent without money or trade, the want of common sustenance, with neither house nor clothes to cover them from the inclemencies of the weather, and the most inevitable prospect of entailing the like or greater miseries upon their breed for ever.

I profess, in the sincerity of my heart, that I have not the least personal interest in endeavoring to promote this necessary work, having no other motive than the public good of my country, by advancing our trade, providing for infants, relieving the poor, and giving some pleasure to the rich. I have no children by which I can propose to get a single penny; the youngest being nine years old, and my wife past childbearing. ³³

7

ARGUING

"SPEECH CODES" ON THE CAMPUS AND PROBLEMS OF FREE SPEECH

Nat Hentoff

During three years of reporting on anti-free-speech tendencies in 1
higher education, I've been at more than twenty colleges and universities—from Washington and Lee and Columbia to Mesa State in Colorado and Stanford.

On this voyage of initially reverse expectations—with liberals 2
fiercely advocating censorship of "offensive" speech and conservatives merrily taking the moral high ground as champions of free expression—the most dismaying moment of revelation took place at Stanford.

An Ecumenical Call for a Harsh Code

In the course of a two-year debate on whether Stanford, like 3
many other universities, should have a speech code punishing language that might wound minorities, women, and gays, a letter appeared in the *Stanford Daily*. Signed by the African-American Law Students Association, the Asian-American Law Students Association, and the Jewish Law Students Association, the letter called for a harsh code. It reflected the letter and the spirit of an earlier declaration by Canetta Ivy, a black leader of student government at Stanford during the period of the great debate. "We don't put as many restrictions on freedom of speech," she said, "as we should."

Reading the letter by this rare ecumenical body of law students 4
(so pressing was the situation that even Jews were allowed in), I

thought of twenty, thirty years from now. From so bright a cadre of graduates, from so prestigious a law school would come some of the law professors, civic leaders, college presidents, and even maybe a Supreme Court justice of the future. And many of them would have learned—like so many other university students in the land—that censorship is okay provided your motives are okay.

The debate at Stanford ended when the president, Donald 5 Kennedy, following the prevailing winds, surrendered his previous position that once you start telling people what they can't say, you will end up telling them what they can't think. Stanford now has a speech code.

This is not to say that these gags on speech—every one of them 6 so overboard and vague that a student can violate a code without knowing he or she has done so—are invariably imposed by student demand. At most colleges, it is the administration that sets up the code. Because there have been racist or sexist or homophobic taunts, anonymous notes or graffiti, the administration feels it must *do something*. The cheapest, quickest way to demonstrate that it cares is to appear to suppress racist, sexist, homophobic speech.

"The Pall of Orthodoxy"

Usually, the leading opposition among the faculty consists of 7 conservatives—when there is opposition. An exception at Stanford was law professor Gerald Gunther, arguably the nation's leading authority on constitutional law. But Gunther did not have much support among other faculty members, conservative or liberal.

At the University of Buffalo Law School, which has a code 8 restricting speech, I could find just one faculty member who was against it. A liberal, he spoke only on condition that I not use his name. He did not want to be categorized as a racist.

On another campus, a political science professor, for whom I had 9 great respect after meeting and talking with him years ago, has been silent—students told me—on what Justice William Brennan once called "the pall of orthodoxy" that has fallen on his campus.

When I talked to him, the professor said, "It doesn't happen in 10 my class. There's no 'politically correct' orthodoxy here. It may happen in other places at this university, but I don't know about that." He said no more.

One of the myths about the rise of P.C. (politically correct) is that, 11 coming from the left, it is primarily intimidating conservatives on campus. Quite the contrary. At almost every college I've been, conservative students have their own newspaper, usually quite lively and fired by a muckraking glee at exposing "politically correct" follies on campus.

By and large, those most intimidated—not so much by the speech codes themselves but by the Madame Defarge–like spirit behind them—are liberal students and those who can be called politically moderate. 12

I've talked to many of them, and they no longer get involved in class discussions when their views would go against the grain of P.C. righteousness. Many, for instance, have questions about certain kinds of affirmative action. They are not partisans of Jesse Helms or David Duke, but they wonder whether progeny of middle-class black families should get scholarship preference. Others have a question about abortion. Most are not pro-life, but they believe that fathers should have a say in whether the fetus should be sent off into eternity. 13

Self-Censorship

Jeff Shesol, a recent graduate of Brown and now a Rhodes scholar at Oxford, became nationally known while at Brown because of his comic strip, "Thatch," which, not too kindly, parodied P.C. students. At a forum on free speech at Brown before he left, Shesol said he wished he could tell the new students at Brown to have no fear of speaking freely. But he couldn't tell them that, he said, advising the new students to stay clear of talking critically about affirmative action or abortion, among other things, in public. 14

At that forum, Shesol told me, he said that those members of the left who regard dissent from their views as racist and sexist should realize that they are discrediting their goals. "They're honorable goals," said Shesol, "and I agree with them. I'm against racism and sexism. But these people's tactics are obscuring the goals. And they've resulted in Brown's no longer being an open-minded place." There were hisses from the audience. 15

Students at New York University Law School have also told me that they censor themselves in class. The kind of chilling atmosphere they describe was exemplified as a case assigned for a moot court competition became subject to denunciation when a sizable number of law students said it was too "offensive" and would hurt the feelings of gay and lesbian students. The case concerned a divorced father's attempt to gain custody of his children on the grounds that 16 their mother had become a lesbian. It was against P.C. to represent the father.

Although some of the faculty responded by insisting that you 17 learn to be a lawyer by dealing with all kinds of cases, including those you personally find offensive, other faculty members supported the rebellious students, praising them for their sensitivity. There was little public opposition from the other students to the attempt to suppress the case. A leading dissenter was a member of the conservative Federalist Society.

What is P.C. to white students is not necessarily P.C. to black stu- 18 dents. Most of the latter did not get involved in the N.Y.U. protest, but throughout the country many black students do support speech codes. A vigorous exception was a black Harvard law school student during a debate on whether the law school should start punishing speech. A white student got up and said that the codes are necessary because without them, black students would be driven away from colleges and thereby deprived of the equal opportunity to get an education.

A black student rose and said that the white student had a hell of 19 a nerve to assume that he—in the face of racist speech—would pack up his books and go home. He's been familiar with that kind of speech all his life, and he had never felt the need to run away from it. He'd handled it before and he could again.

The black student then looked at his white colleague and said 20 that it was condescending to say that blacks have to be "protected" from racist speech. "It is more racist and insulting," he emphasized, "to say that to me than to call me a nigger."

But that would appear to be a minority view among black stu- 21 dents. Most are convinced they do need to be protected from wounding language. On the other hand, a good many black student organizations on campus do not feel that Jews have to be protected from wounding language.

Presence of Anti-Semitism

Though it's not much written about in reports of the language 22 wars on campus, there is a strong strain of anti-Semitism among some—not all, by any means—black students. They invite such speakers as Louis Farrakhan, the former Stokely Carmichael (now Kwame Touré), and such lesser but still burning bushes as Steve Cokely, the Chicago commentator who has declared that Jewish doctors inject the AIDS virus into black babies. That distinguished leader was invited to speak at the University of Michigan.

The black student organization at Columbia University brought 23 to the campus Dr. Khallid Abdul Muhammad. He began his address by saying: "My leader, my teacher, my guide is the honorable Louis Farrakhan. I thought that should be said at Columbia Jewniversity."

Many Jewish students have not censored themselves in reacting 24 to this form of political correctness among some blacks. A Columbia student, Rachel Stoll, wrote a letter to the *Columbia Spectator:* "I have an idea. As a white Jewish American, I'll just stand in the middle of a circle comprising . . . Khallid Abdul Muhammad and assorted members of the Black Students Organization and let them all hurl large stones at me. From recent events and statements made on this campus, I gather this will be a good cheap method of making these people feel good."

At UCLA, a black student magazine printed an article indicating 25 there is considerable truth to the *Protocols of the Elders of Zion.*[1] For months, the black faculty, when asked their reactions, preferred not to comment. One of them did say that the black students already considered the black faculty to be insufficiently militant, and the professors didn't want to make the gap any wider. Like white liberal faculty members on other campuses, they want to be liked—or at least not too disliked.

Along with quiet white liberal faculty members, most black professors have not opposed the speech codes. But unlike the white liberals many honestly do believe that minority students have to be insulated from barbed language. They do not believe—as I have found out in a number of conversations—that an essential part of an education is to learn to demystify language, to strip it of its ability to demonize and stigmatize you. They do not believe that the way to deal with bigoted language is to answer it with more and better language of your own. This seems very elementary to me, but not to the defenders, black and white, of the speech codes.

"Fighting Words"

Consider University of California president David Gardner. He 27 has imposed a speech code on all the campuses in his university sys-

---

[1] *Protocols of the Elders of Zion:* a document forged c. 1897 alleging that an international Jewish conspiracy was plotting the overthrow of Christian civilization.

tem. Students are to be punished—and this is characteristic of the other codes around the country—if they use "fighting words"— derogatory references to "race, sex, sexual orientation, or disability."

The term "fighting words" comes from a 1942 Supreme Court 28 decision, *Chaplinsky v. New Hampshire,* which ruled that "fighting words" are not protected by the First Amendment. That decision, however, has been in disuse at the High Court for many years. But it is thriving on college campuses.

In the California code, a word becomes "fighting" if it is directly 29 addressed to "any ordinary person" (presumably, extraordinary people are above all this). These are the kinds of words that are "inherently likely to provoke a violent action, *whether or not they actually do."* (Emphasis added.)

Moreover, he or she who fires a fighting word at any ordinary 30 person can be reprimanded or dismissed from the university because the perpetrator should "reasonably know" that what he or she has said will interfere with the "victim's ability to pursue effectively his or her education or otherwise participate fully in university programs and activities."

Asked Gary Murikami, chairman of the Gay and Lesbian 31 Association at the University of California, Berkeley: "What does it mean?"

Among those—faculty, law professors, college administrators— 32 who insist such codes are essential to the university's purpose of making *all* students feel at home and thereby able to concentrate on their work, there has been a celebratory resort to the Fourteenth Amendment.

That amendment guarantees "equal protection of the laws" to 33 all, and that means to all students on campus. Accordingly, when the First Amendment rights of those engaging in offensive speech clash with the equality rights of their targets under the Fourteenth Amendment, the First Amendment must give way.

This is the thesis, by the way, of John Powell, legal director of the 34 American Civil Liberties Union, even though that organization has now formally opposed all college speech codes—after a considerable civil war among and within its affiliates.

The battle of the amendments continues, and when harsher 35 codes are called for at some campuses, you can expect the Fourteenth Amendment—which was not intended to censor *speech*—will rise again.

A precedent has been set at, of all places, colleges and universi- 36 ties, that the principle of free speech is merely situational. As college administrators change, so will the extent of free speech on campus. And invariably, permissible speech will become more and more narrowly defined. Once speech can be limited in such subjective ways, more and more expression will be included in what is forbidden.

Freedom of Thought

One of the exceedingly few college presidents who speaks out on 37 the consequences of the anti-free-speech movement is Yale University's Benno Schmidt:

> Freedom of thought must be Yale's central commitment. It is not easy to embrace. It is, indeed, the effort of a lifetime. . . . Much expression that is free may deserve our contempt. We may well be moved to exercise our own freedom to counter it or to ignore it. But universities cannot censor or suppress speech, no matter how obnoxious in content, without violating their justification for existence. . . .

> On some other campuses in this country, values of civility and community have been offered by some as paramount values of the university, even to the extent of superseding freedom of expression.

> Such a view is wrong in principle and, if extended, is disastrous to freedom of thought. . . . The chilling effects on speech of the vagueness and open-ended nature of many universities' prohibitions . . . are compounded by the fact that these codes are typically enforced by faculty and students who commonly assert that vague notions of community are more important to the academy than freedom of thought and expression. . . .

> This is a flabby and uncertain time for freedom in the United States.

On the Public Broadcasting System in June 1991, I was part of a 38 Fred Friendly panel at Stanford University in a debate on speech codes versus freedom of expression. The three black panelists strongly supported the codes. So did the one Asian-American on the panel. But then so did Stanford law professor Thomas Grey, who wrote the Stanford code, and Stanford president Donald Kennedy, who first opposed and then embraced the code. We have a new ecumenicism of those who would control speech for the greater good. It is hardly a new idea, but the mix of advocates is rather new.

But there are other voices. In the national board debate at the 39
ACLU on college speech codes, the first speaker—and I think she had
a lot to do with making the final vote against codes unanimous—was
Gwen Thomas.

A black community college administrator from Colorado, she is 40
a fiercely persistent exposer of racial discrimination.

She started by saying, "I have always felt as a minority person 41
that we have to protect the rights of all because if we infringe on the
rights of any persons, we'll be next.

"As for providing a nonintimidating educational environment, 42
our young people have to learn to grow up on college campuses. We
have to teach them how to deal with adversarial situations. They
have to learn how to survive offensive speech they find wounding
and hurtful." Gwen Thomas is an educator—an endangered species
in higher education.

THE FREE-SPEECH FOLLIES

Stanley Fish

The modern American version of crying wolf is crying First 1
Amendment. If you want to burn a cross on a black family's lawn or
buy an election by contributing millions to a candidate or vilify Jerry
Falwell and his mother in a scurrilous "parody," and someone or
some government agency tries to stop you, just yell "First
Amendment rights" and you will stand a good chance of getting to
do what you want to do.

In the academy, the case is even worse: Not only is the First 2
Amendment pressed into service at the drop of a hat (especially
whenever anyone is disciplined for anything), it is invoked ritually
when there are no First Amendment issues in sight.

Take the case of the editors of college newspapers who will 3
always cry First Amendment when something they've published
turns out to be the cause of outrage and controversy. These days the
offending piece or editorial or advertisement usually involves (what
is at least perceived to be) an attack on Jews. In January of this year,
the *Daily Illini*, a student newspaper at the University of Illinois at
Urbana-Champaign, printed a letter from a resident of Seattle with
no university affiliation. The letter ran under the headline "Jews
Manipulate America" and argued that because their true allegiance is
to the state of Israel, the president should "separate Jews from all
government advisory positions"; otherwise, the writer warned, "the
Jews might face another Holocaust."

When the predictable firestorm of outrage erupted, the newspa- 4
per's editor responded by declaring, first, that "we are committed to
giving all people a voice"; second, that, given this commitment, "we
print the opinions of others with whom we do not agree"; third, that
to do otherwise would involve the newspaper in the dangerous acts
of "silencing" and "self-censorship"; and, fourth, that "what is hate
speech to one member of a society is free speech to another."

Wrong four times. 5

I'll bet the *Daily Illini* is not committed to giving all people a 6
voice—the KKK? man-boy love? advocates of slavery? would-be
Unabombers? Nor do I believe that the editors sift through submis-
sions looking for the ones they disagree with and then print those.
No doubt they apply some principles of selection, asking questions

like, Is it relevant, or Is it timely, or Does it get the facts right, or Does it present a coherent argument?

That is, they exercise judgment, which is quite a different thing 7 from silencing or self-censorship. No one is silenced because a single outlet declines to publish him; silencing occurs when that outlet (or any other) is forbidden by the state to publish him on pain of legal action; and that is also what censorship is.

As for self-censoring, if it is anything, it is what we all do when- 8 ever we decide it would be better not to say something or cut a sentence that went just a little bit too far or leave a manuscript in the bottom drawer because it is not yet ready. Self-censorship, in short, is not a crime or a moral failing; it is a responsibility.

And, finally, whatever the merits of the argument by which all 9 assertions are relativised—your hate speech is my free speech—this incident has nothing to do with either hate speech or free speech and everything to do with whether the editors are discharging or defaulting on their obligations when they foist them off on an inapplicable doctrine, saying in effect, "The First Amendment made us do it."

More recently, the same scenario played itself out at Santa Rosa 10 Junior College. This time it was a student who wrote the offending article. Titled "Is Anti-Semitism Ever the Result of Jewish Behavior?" it answered the question in the affirmative, creating an uproar that included death threats, an avalanche of hate mail, and demands for just about everyone's resignation. The faculty adviser who had approved the piece said, "The First Amendment isn't there to protect agreeable stories."

He was alluding to the old saw that the First Amendment pro- 11 tects unpopular as well as popular speech. But what it protects unpopular speech from is abridgment by the government of its free expression; it does not protect unpopular speech from being rejected by a newspaper, and it confers no positive obligation to give your pages over to unpopular speech, or popular speech, or any speech.

Once again, there is no First Amendment issue here, just an issue 12 of editorial judgment and the consequences of exercising it. (You can print anything you like; but if the heat comes, it's yours, not the Constitution's.)

In these controversies, student editors are sometimes portrayed, 13 or portray themselves, as First Amendment heroes who bravely risk criticism and censure in order to uphold a cherished American value. But they are not heroes; they are merely confused and, in terms of their understanding of the doctrine they invoke, rather hapless.

Not as hapless, however, as the Harvard English department, 14 which made a collective fool of itself three times when it invited, disinvited and then reinvited poet Tom Paulin to be the Morris Gray lecturer. Again the flash point was anti-Semitism. In his poetry and in public comments, Paulin had said that Israel had no right to exist, that settlers on the West Bank "should be shot dead," and that Israeli police and military forces were the equivalent of the Nazi SS. When these and other statements came to light shortly before Paulin was to give his lecture, the department voted to rescind the invitation. When the inevitable cry of "censorship, censorship" was heard in the land, the department flip-flopped again, and a professor-spokesman declared, "This was a clear affirmation that the department stood strongly by the First Amendment."

It was of course nothing of the kind; it was a transparent effort of 15 a bunch that had already put its foot in its mouth twice to wriggle out of trouble and regain the moral high ground by striking the pose of First Amendment defender. But, in fact, the department and its members were not First Amendment defenders (a religion they converted to a little late), but serial bunglers.

What should they have done? Well, it depends on what they 16 wanted to do. If they wanted to invite this particular poet because they admired his poetry, they had a perfect right to do so. If they were aware ahead of time of Paulin's public pronouncements, they could have chosen either to say something by way of explanation or to remain silent and let the event speak for itself; either course of action would have been at once defensible and productive of risk. If they knew nothing of Paulin's anti-Israel sentiments (difficult to believe of a gang of world-class researchers) but found out about them after the fact, they might have said, "Oops, never mind" or toughed it out—again alternatives not without risk. But at each stage, whatever they did or didn't do would have had no relationship whatsoever to any First Amendment right—Paulin had no right to be invited—or obligation—there was no obligation either to invite or disinvite him, and certainly no obligation to reinvite him, unless you count the obligations imposed on yourself by a succession of ill-thought-through decisions. Whatever the successes or failures here, they were once again failures of judgment, not doctrine.

In another case, it looked for a moment that judgment of an 17 appropriate kind was in fact being exercised. The University of California at Berkeley houses the Emma Goldman Papers Project, and each year the director sends out a fund-raising mailer that always features quotations from Goldman's work. But this January an associate vice chancellor edited the mailer and removed two quotations that in context read as a criticism of the Bush administration's plans for a war in Iraq. He explained that the quotations were not randomly chosen and were clearly intended to make a "political point, and that is inappropriate in an official university situation."

The project director (who acknowledged that the quotes were 18 selected for their contemporary relevance) objected to what she saw as an act of censorship and a particularly egregious one given Goldman's strong advocacy of free expression.

But no one's expression was being censored. The Goldman quo- 19 tations are readily available and had they appeared in the project's literature in a setting that did not mark them as political, no concerns would have been raised. It is just, said the associate vice chancellor, that they are inappropriate in this context, and, he added, "It is not a matter of the First Amendment."

Right, it's a matter of whether or not there is even the appearance 20 of the university's taking sides on a partisan issue; that is, it is an empirical matter that requires just the exercise of judgment that associate vice chancellors are paid to perform. Of course he was pilloried by members of the Berkeley faculty and others who saw First Amendment violations everywhere.

But there were none. Goldman still speaks freely through her 21 words. The project director can still make her political opinions known by writing letters to the editor or to everyone in the country, even if she cannot use the vehicle of a university flier to do so. Everyone's integrity is preserved. The project goes on unimpeded, and the university goes about its proper academic business. Or so it would have been had the administration stayed firm. But it folded and countermanded the associate vice chancellor's decision.

At least the chancellor had sense enough to acknowledge that no 22 one's speech had been abridged. It was just, he said, an "error in judgment." Aren't they all?

Are there then no free-speech issues on campuses? Sure there are; 23 there just aren't very many. When Toni Smith, a basketball player at Manhattanville College, turned her back to the flag during the playing of the national anthem in protest against her government's policies, she was truly exercising her First Amendment rights, rights that ensure that she cannot be compelled to an affirmation she does not endorse (see *West Virginia v. Barnette*). And as she stood by her principles in the face of hostility, she truly was (and is) a First Amendment hero, as the college newspaper editors, the members of the Harvard English department, and the head of the Emma Goldman Project are not. The category is a real one, and it would be good if it were occupied only by those who belong in it.

IT'S TIME TO JUNK THE DOUBLE STANDARD ON FREE SPEECH

Stuart Taylor Jr.

It made news when hecklers booed *Sacramento Bee* publisher 1
Janis Besler Heaphy so loudly and long—for suggesting that the government had gone too far in curbing civil liberties since September 11—that she could not finish her December 15 commencement speech at California State University (Sacramento). "Many interpret it as a troubling example of rising intolerance for public discourse that questions the nation's response to the September 11 terror attacks," reported the *Los Angeles Times*. *The New York Times* and other major newspapers weighed in with similar articles. ABC News' *Nightline* did a special report.

Another burst of publicity—and more worries about threats to 2
First Amendment rights—attended the University of New Mexico's reprimand of professor Richard Berthold for opening his September 11 history class with what he later admitted to be a "stupid" remark: "Anyone who can blow up the Pentagon gets my vote." Berthold also received death threats.

It's nice to see the media showing some concern for the freedom 3
of speech. But where have they been during the past two decades of efforts coming from the politically correct Left—and especially from devotees of identity politics, racial preferences, and the male-bashing brand of feminism—to suppress unwelcome speech on our campuses and elsewhere? Examples:

- Ward Connerly, the black California businessman who has campaigned across the nation to outlaw racial preferences, has been shouted down and drowned out so abusively as to cut short his remarks on at least five campuses since 1996, he recalls, including Atlanta's Emory University in 1998 and the University of Texas School of Law in 1999. The consequence, he says, is that "it totally throws you off your stride. Freedom of speech is not just being able to complete your speech, it's being able to speak without fear of personal harm being done to you. . . . I am not free to speak openly and honestly." College administrators, Connerly adds, "almost go out of their way to make me out as a monster, which incites the audience all the more." Taunts of "Uncle Tom" are routine and, more than once, Connerly notes, hecklers have

115

threatened violence or announced menacingly, "We know where you live."

- Linda Chavez, another leading critic of racial preferences, says: "I have been disinvited, harassed, shouted down, threatened, and [on one occasion] physically assaulted at campuses around the country," including the University of Northern Colorado and the University of Illinois (Urbana-Champaign). Chavez says that while the most-menacing hecklers appeared to be "street thugs" brought in from outside the campuses, students who join in "are being primed by the professors, being told that I'm the devil incarnate, that I want to do terrible things to Hispanics."

- Christina Hoff Sommers, a trenchant critic of liberal feminism, was speaking as an invited panelist at a November 1 conference on preventing substance abuse, organized by the Health and Human Services Department, when some officials, academics, and others took offense at her doubts about a program called "Girl Power." A department official named Linda Bass interrupted and angrily ordered Sommers to stop talking about Girl Power. Later, Sommers said, Fordham University psychology professor (and paid department consultant) Jay Wade told Sommers, "Shut the f- up, bitch," amid mocking laughter from the crowd. Sommers, effectively silenced, left. "As Stanley Kurtz pointed out in *National Review*," Sommers notes, "if Catharine MacKinnon or Carol Gilligan had been treated that way in a government meeting, it would have been reported." Very widely.

But none of these efforts to silence Connerly, Chavez, and 4 Sommers by heckler's veto has ever been reported in any national newspaper, as far as I can find, excepting some coverage in the conservative *Washington Times*, a few opinion columns, *Wall Street Journal* editorials, and a passing mention of Connerly's complaint deep in *The New York Times*. Nor have the national media paid much attention to the pervasive use of speech codes to chill politically incorrect expression on campus. They have likewise ignored the long-running epidemic of thefts of campus newspapers for carrying politically incorrect commentary or advertisements.

"University PR and spin has led too many of the media into a ter- 5 rible double standard" in dealing with such heckler's vetoes and other forms of censorship, says Thor L. Halvorssen, executive director of the Foundation for Individual Rights in Education Inc. (FIRE). "When it's a conservative [being shouted down], the university will downplay this as a free speech protest, and the media will agree."

The Philadelphia-based FIRE was created two years ago by 6
Boston civil liberties lawyer Harvey Silverglate and University of
Pennsylvania professor Alan Charles Kors to protect free speech and
other liberties on the nation's campuses. And Halvorssen seethes
with the same passionate indignation in denouncing censorial efforts
coming from the political Right as those from the Left. But before
September 11, he says, the campus censorship came mostly from the
Left. And the big media were not interested.

"Close to three-quarters of the colleges and universities, private 7
and public, have speech codes," Halvorssen stresses. "They are
applied selectively, with a double standard depending on your blood
and culture. I've never heard of a case of anyone being suspended or
fired or expelled for insulting a born-again Christian. On a college
campus, Andres Serrano's photograph of a crucifix in urine, titled
Piss Christ, is a work of art. Immerse a photograph of Martin Luther
King Jr. in urine, and the sky would fall and the entire school would
be put through sensitivity training. There is also a ferocious assault
on due process and fairness on campus."

Administrators mete out discipline for offending remarks, for 8
other alleged "harassment," and even for disputed charges of date
rape with no semblance of a fair hearing. "We hear a lot of people
talking about military tribunals," Halvorssen notes. "We have the
equivalent on campus. . . . I see this stuff on a daily basis, and it is a
real struggle to get it into the media. Speech codes, thought reform,
due process—where have these folks been?"

Since September 11, with leftist critics of the war against terror- 9
ism complaining of efforts to intimidate and punish them both on
campus and elsewhere, the media have paid a bit more attention-
although, Halvorssen says, "it's the equivalent of reporting on how
many people are getting into the boats rather than reporting that the
Titanic is sinking." The coverage has also been more balanced, if only
because it would be hard to chronicle the punitive measures against
anti-war leftists and Islamists without noticing that, on the campuses, efforts to silence forcefully hawkish statements deemed offensive by Muslims seem about as common.

The reporting on the Berthold "blow up the Pentagon" case, for 10
example, has been paralleled by extensive coverage of a case at
Orange Coast College in California in which Professor Kenneth
Hearlson was suspended for 11 weeks without a hearing and threatened with dismissal after four Muslim students complained that he
had called them terrorists and murderers in class. When other students produced tape-recordings proving this charge to be false, the

college reprimanded Hearlson anyway, for accusing Muslims in general of condoning terrorism against Israel.

Meanwhile, the University of South Florida is seeking to fire 11 Sami Al-Arian—a tenured Palestinian professor of computer science who is suspected (but not formally accused) of links to Islamic extremists—for courting publicity (amid dozens of death threats) about his views and controversial past. On the other end of the spectrum, a library assistant at UCLA was suspended for a week without pay for calling Israel an "apartheid state" in an e-mail. An Ethiopian student at San Diego State University was warned that he could be suspended or expelled for "harassment" after he had confronted and criticized a group of Saudi students for celebrating the destruction of the World Trade Center. And so on.

Many campus administrators, notes Halvorssen, bend according 12 to "where the political winds are blowing." And now that some of the winds are blowing against the Left, even on a lot of campuses, the left-liberal *Nation* sees the danger. "The last generation's wave of campus speech codes and anti-harassment policies," wrote David Glenn in December, "may have done more to suppress freedom than to remedy injustice in any meaningful way-and it may be only now, after September 11, that the full costs will become apparent."

The rediscovery, by some in the media and the Left, of the case 13 for free speech makes FIRE's Halvorssen optimistic about the future. But will politically powerful conservatives—some of whom have become First Amendment stalwarts while seeing their own oxes gored by campus censors—prove equally selective in their devotion to free speech? "We have to be careful," says Christina Hoff Sommers, "not to play by the rules written by the intolerant Left."

A CHILL WIND IS BLOWING IN THIS NATION

Tim Robbins

I can't tell you how moved I have been at the overwhelming support I have received from newspapers throughout the country in these past few days. I hold no illusions that all of these journalists agree with me on my views against the war. While the journalists' outrage at the cancellation of our appearance in Cooperstown is not about my views, it is about my right to express these views. I am extremely grateful that there are those of you out there still with a fierce belief in constitutionally guaranteed rights. We need you, the press, now more than ever. This is a crucial moment for all of us.

For all of the ugliness and tragedy of 9/11, there was a brief period afterward where I held a great hope, in the midst of the tears and shocked faces of New Yorkers, in the midst of the lethal air we breathed as we worked at Ground Zero, in the midst of my children's terror at being so close to this crime against humanity, in the midst of all this, I held on to a glimmer of hope in the naive assumption that something good could come out of it.

I imagined our leaders seizing upon this moment of unity in America, this moment when no one wanted to talk about Democrat versus Republican, white versus black, or any of the other ridiculous divisions that dominate our public discourse. I imagined our leaders going on television telling the citizens that although we all want to be at Ground Zero, we can't, but there is work that is needed to be done all over America. Our help is needed at community centers to tutor children, to teach them to read. Our work is needed at old-age homes to visit the lonely and infirmed; in gutted neighborhoods to rebuild housing and clean up parks, and convert abandoned lots to baseball fields. I imagined leadership that would take this incredible energy, this generosity of spirit and create a new unity in America born out of the chaos and tragedy of 9/11, a new unity that would send a message to terrorists everywhere: If you attack us, we will become stronger, cleaner, better educated, and more unified. You will strengthen our commitment to justice and democracy by your inhumane attacks on us. Like a Phoenix out of the fire, we will be reborn.

And then came the speech: You are either with us or against us. And the bombing began. And the old paradigm was restored as our leader encouraged us to show our patriotism by shopping and by volunteering to join groups that would turn in their neighbor for any suspicious behavior.

In the 19 months since 9/11, we have seen our democracy com- 5
promised by fear and hatred. Basic inalienable rights, due process,
the sanctity of the home have been quickly compromised in a climate
of fear. A unified American public has grown bitterly divided, and a
world population that had profound sympathy and support for us
has grown contemptuous and distrustful, viewing us as we once
viewed the Soviet Union, as a rogue state.

This past weekend, Susan and I and the three kids went to 6
Florida for a family reunion of sorts. Amidst the alcohol and the
dancing, sugar-rushing children, there was, of course, talk of the war.
And the most frightening thing about the weekend was the amount
of times we were thanked for speaking out against the war because
that individual speaking thought it unsafe to do so in their own community, in their own life. Keep talking, they said; I haven't been able
to open my mouth.

A relative tells me that a history teacher tells his 11-year-old son, 7
my nephew, that Susan Sarandon is endangering the troops by her
opposition to the war. Another teacher in a different school asks our
niece if we are coming to the school play. They're not welcome here,
said the molder of young minds.

Another relative tells me of a school board decision to cancel a 8
civics event that was proposing to have a moment of silence for those
who have died in the war because the students were including dead
Iraqi civilians in their silent prayer.

A teacher in another nephew's school is fired for wearing a 9
T-shirt with a peace sign on it. And a friend of the family tells of listening to the radio down South as the talk radio host calls for the
murder of a prominent anti-war activist. Death threats have
appeared on other prominent anti-war activists' doorsteps for their
views. Relatives of ours have received threatening e-mails and phone
calls. And my 13-year-old boy, who has done nothing to anybody, has
recently been embarrassed and humiliated by a sadistic creep who
writes—or, rather, scratches his column with his fingernails in dirt.

Susan and I have been listed as traitors, as supporters of Saddam, 10
and various other epithets by the Aussie gossip rags masquerading
as newspapers, and by their fair and balanced electronic media
cousins, 19th Century Fox. (Laughter.) Apologies to Gore Vidal.
(Applause.)

Two weeks ago, the United Way canceled Susan's appearance at 11
a conference on women's leadership. And both of us last week were
told that both we and the First Amendment were not welcome at the
Baseball Hall of Fame.

A famous middle-aged rock-and-roller called me last week to 12 thank me for speaking out against the war, only to go on to tell me that he could not speak himself because he fears repercussions from Clear Channel. "They promote our concert appearances," he said. "They own most of the stations that play our music. I can't come out against this war."

And here in Washington, Helen Thomas finds herself banished 13 to the back of the room and uncalled on after asking Ari Fleischer whether our showing prisoners of war at Guantanamo Bay on television violated the Geneva Convention.

A chill wind is blowing in this nation. A message is being sent 14 through the White House and its allies in talk radio and Clear Channel and Cooperstown. If you oppose this administration, there can and will be ramifications.

Every day, the air waves are filled with warnings, veiled and 15 unveiled threats, spewed invective and hatred directed at any voice of dissent. And the public, like so many relatives and friends that I saw this weekend, sit in mute opposition and fear.

I am sick of hearing about Hollywood being against this war. 16 Hollywood's heavy hitters, the real power brokers and cover-of-the-magazine stars, have been largely silent on this issue. But Hollywood, the concept, has always been a popular target.

I remember when the Columbine High School shootings hap- 17 pened. President Clinton criticized Hollywood for contributing to this terrible tragedy—this, as we were dropping bombs over Kosovo. Could the violent actions of our leaders contribute somewhat to the violent fantasies of our teenagers? Or is it all just Hollywood and rock and roll?

I remember reading at the time that one of the shooters had tried 18 to enlist to fight the real war a week before he acted out his war in real life at Columbine. I talked about this in the press at the time. And curiously, no one accused me of being unpatriotic for criticizing Clinton. In fact, the same radio patriots that call us traitors today engaged in daily personal attacks on their president during the war in Kosovo.

Today, prominent politicians who have decried violence in 19 movies—the "Blame Hollywooders," if you will—recently voted to give our current president the power to unleash real violence in our current war. They want us to stop the fictional violence but are okay with the real kind.

And these same people that tolerate the real violence of war 20 don't want to see the result of it on the nightly news. Unlike the rest of the world, our news coverage of this war remains sanitized, without a glimpse of the blood and gore inflicted upon our soldiers or the women and children in Iraq. Violence as a concept, an abstraction—it's very strange.

As we applaud the hard-edged realism of the opening battle   21
scene of "Saving Private Ryan," we cringe at the thought of seeing the same on the nightly news. We are told it would be pornographic. We want no part of reality in real life. We demand that war be painstakingly realized on the screen, but that war remain imagined and conceptualized in real life.

And in the midst of all this madness, where is the political oppo-   22
sition? Where have all the Democrats gone? Long time passing, long time ago. (Applause.) With apologies to Robert Byrd, I have to say it is pretty embarrassing to live in a country where a five-foot-one comedian has more guts than most politicians. (Applause.) We need leaders, not pragmatists that cower before the spin zones of former entertainment journalists. We need leaders who can understand the Constitution, congressman who don't in a moment of fear abdicate their most important power, the right to declare war to the executive branch. And, please, can we please stop the congressional sing-a-longs? (Laughter.)

In this time when a citizenry applauds the liberation of a country   23
as it lives in fear of its own freedom, when an administration official releases an attack ad questioning the patriotism of a legless Vietnam veteran running for Congress, when people all over the country fear reprisal if they use their right to free speech, it is time to get angry. It is time to get fierce. And it doesn't take much to shift the tide. My 11-year-old nephew, mentioned earlier, a shy kid who never talks in class, stood up to his history teacher who was questioning Susan's patriotism. "That's my aunt you're talking about. Stop it." And the stunned teacher backtracks and began stammering compliments in embarrassment.

Sportswriters across the country reacted with such overwhelm-   24
ing fury at the Hall of Fame that the president of the Hall admitted he made a mistake and Major League Baseball disavowed any connection to the actions of the Hall's president. A bully can be stopped, and so can a mob. It takes one person with the courage and a resolute voice.

The journalists in this country can battle back at those who   25
would rewrite our Constitution in Patriot Act II, or "Patriot, The Sequel," as we would call it in Hollywood. We are counting on you to star in that movie. Journalists can insist that they not be used as

publicists by this administration. (Applause.) The next White House correspondent to be called on by Ari Fleischer should defer their question to the back of the room, to the banished journalist du jour. (Applause.) And any instance of intimidation to free speech should be battled against. Any acquiescence or intimidation at this point will only lead to more intimidation. You have, whether you like it or not, an awesome responsibility and an awesome power: the fate of discourse, the health of this republic is in your hands, whether you write on the left or the right. This is your time, and the destiny you have chosen.

We lay the continuance of our democracy on your desks, and 26 count on your pens to be mightier. Millions are watching and waiting in mute frustration and hope—hoping for someone to defend the spirit and letter of our Constitution, and to defy the intimidation that is visited upon us daily in the name of national security and warped notions of patriotism.

Our ability to disagree, and our inherent right to question our 27 leaders and criticize their actions define who we are. To allow those rights to be taken away out of fear, to punish people for their beliefs, to limit access in the news media to differing opinions is to acknowledge our democracy's defeat. These are challenging times. There is a wave of hate that seeks to divide us—right and left, pro-war and anti-war. In the name of my 11-year-old nephew, and all the other unreported victims of this hostile and unproductive environment of fear, let us try to find our common ground as a nation. Let us celebrate this grand and glorious experiment that has survived for 227 years. To do so we must honor and fight vigilantly for the things that unite us—like freedom, the First Amendment and, yes, baseball. (Applause.)

CREDITS

Sherman J. Alexie, Jr. "The Authorized Autobiography of Me." Reprinted from *One Stick Song* © 2000 by Sherman Alexie, by permission of Hanging Loose Press.

Karen W. Arenson, "Reading Statistical Tea Leaves." *The New York Times*. Copyright © 2001 *The New York Times*. Reprinted by permission.

Roland Barthes, "Toys," from *Mythologies* by Roland Barthes, translated by Annette Lavers. Translation copyright © 1992 by Jonathan Cape, Ltd. Reprinted by permission of Hill and Wang, a division of Farrar, Straus & Giroux, LLC.

Joan Jacobs Brumberg, "The Origins of Anorexia Nervosa," from *Fasting Girls: The Emergence of Anorexia Nervosa as a Modern Disease.* (Cambridge: Harvard University Press, 1988.) Copyright © 1988, 1989 by Joan Jacobs Brumberg. Reprinted by permission of the Georges Borchardt, Inc. for the author.

Fox Butterfield, "Why They Excel," from *PARADE*. Copyright © 1991 Fox Butterfield. Reprinted with the permission of *PARADE* and the author.

Judith Ortiz Cofer, "Marina," from *Silent Dancing: A Partial Remembrance of a Puerto Rican Childhood.* Copyright © 1990 Judith Ortiz Cofer. Reprinted by permission of Arte Publico Press.

Anne Dillard, *"Lenses," from Teaching a Stone to Talk: Expeditions and Encounters.* Copyright © 1982 by Anne Dillard. Reprinted by permission of Harper Collins Publishers, Inc.